P9-BZJ-651

ADELE

ALSO BY MARC SHAPIRO

ADELE

The Biography

MARC SHAPIRO

ST. MARTIN'S GRIFFIN
NEW YORK

www.stmartins.com

Design by Steven Seighman

ISBN 978-1-250-02516-6 (trade paperback)
ISBN 978-1-250-02547-0 (hardcover)
ISBN 978-1-250-02515-9 (e-book)

First Edition: July 2012

10 9 8 7 6 5 4 3 2 1

THIS BOOK IS DEDICATED TO . . .

My wife, Nancy. My daughter, Rachael. My granddaughter, Lily. My son-in-law, Ian. Brady and Fitch. Mike. The guy who delivers my newspaper every morning, and all the real people in my life. My agent, Lori Perkins. Marc Resnick at St. Martin's. Good books, good art, good music. The fantasy and the reality. The time at the party and the time in solitude. And last but certainly not least . . . thanks, Adele, for a story worth telling.

TABLE OF CONTENTS

INTRODUCTION
THE YEAR THAT WAS

2011 would definitely go down as an eventful year for Adele. And by November, nobody could blame the British-born singer for wanting to pull into her shell for some heavy preholiday rest.

Her debut album, 2008's emotionally wrought exercise in soul, blues, and angst, *19*, and a boatload of rave press notices had labeled this young lass, believably cockney to the core and with a penchant for tales of love as a battlefield, as the next *this* and the next *that*.

Comparisons to everybody from Madonna and Amy Winehouse to a modern-day Etta James and all performers in between fell like rain, putting the barely twenty-year-old singer in truly prestigious company and raising the inevitable questions. Questions that, at a time when much of what passed for popular music was cynical, condescending, and worst of all, prefab and devoid of soul, had to be asked.

Could the alternately gregarious and insecure performer

with the bright smile, easygoing nature, honest laugh, and potty mouth overcome the dreaded "next big thing" tag? Would a steady diet of songs bemoaning lost love survive in a world populated by lighter-than-air songs holding momentary space until the next bit of fluff comes along? Could something so simple and to the point work in a world populated by clichés, provocatively dressed performers, and empty, lyrical special effects?

And one more thing: Could Adele, owing more to the past than the present and the future, become the next big thing?

It remained for the January 2011 release of the much-anticipated follow-up, *21*, to cement the idea of Adele as somebody with superstar chops.

21 was as assured and wide-ranging as its predecessor, mixing and matching her evocative, brilliantly accented vocals and passionate, quite personal songwriting with soul, jazz, pop, hip-hop, and yes, even a heartfelt brand of country influences. Adele's modern telling of universal truths was soothing and to the point. People would admit to falling silent and often tearing up when listening to Adele's music. Those who managed to catch the singer in concert came away from the experience feeling they had discovered a kindred spirit.

Not surprisingly, the power of her music continued to spread like wildfire. The songs "Rolling In The Deep," "Someone Like You," and "Set Fire To The Rain" picked up where her previous album's "Chasing Pavements" and "Cold Shoulder" left off as mantras for the new introspective generation.

And it was not just the real people who had taken Adele

into their hearts. The likes of Kanye West, Beyoncé, and Dave Grohl had tweeted her praises and talked her up in interviews. It was not just celebrity BS, the things you say but never mean.

"She doesn't carry any of the baggage of today's pop stars," producer Rick Rubin told *ABC News*. "What she makes is her art and at no time does it feel like product."

"She's a voice, and she's classic. I have great admiration for her," said Dolores O'Riordan of The Cranberries in an interview in *St. Catharine's Standard*.

"She's got a beautiful voice," Dave Grohl of the Foo Fighters told Digital Spy. "People are shocked when they hear actual talent."

People see Adele as someone very real with the potential to be timeless.

Indeed, Adele's songs were certainly not just of the moment. From the spare, tough instrumentals to Adele's haunting, soulful vocal refrains, there is something that defies a sense of the "here and now and gone tomorrow." Even the hippest modern technological touches take a backseat to the basics. Once upon a time, when the lights were down low in a smoky club and an audience sat enraptured amid the soft clinking of glasses, this is how music that would last sounded.

At the height of Adele's notoriety, the most jaded of critics hinted at the notion that Adele's songs were standards in the making. Like the great ladies of preceding generations—Fitzgerald, Franklin, Holiday, and James—Adele's sense of stylistic intimacy was the kind of music that would, most assuredly, be played forever. Because there would always be an audience for it. The likes of "Rolling In The Deep" and

"Chasing Pavements" were songs that listeners would be proud to suggest for the next generation.

21's reception and the at-large impact Adele's brand of soul music seemed to be having on her fans and fellow performers alike has always been a concept that she could not completely make sense of. "People take some comfort in my songs," she said in a *People* piece, "and that's the most amazing thing."

Over the course of two albums, Adele had turned the idea of lost love and heartbreak into art, something that just made sense to an audience who knew what those emotions were all about, but who had seen many modern artists play fast and loose with those emotions.

The album would sell more than 17 million copies worldwide in the first year and would make Adele the biggest-selling artist of 2011. Sales records fell like so many dominos. She was leaving legends like The Beatles, Madonna, Prince, and Pink Floyd and current fave Lady Gaga in her wake.

It was a dream come true. But then the nightmare kicked in.

Shortly after the album's release, Adele was on a promotional tour of Europe when, during a stopover in Paris, she suddenly lost her voice.

"I was right in the middle of singing when, all of a sudden, my voice just popped and it was gone," she said in a 2011 *60 Minutes* interview. "At that point I probably should have stopped singing for at least six months."

But the incident was dismissed as laryngitis and quickly relegated to the price one occasionally pays when you've been singing near nonstop since childhood.

Not so easily dismissed was the blood vessel that burst in her vocal cords during a May concert trip to America. For Adele and her handlers, this was much more serious than laryngitis. Adele returned to London and the injury healed.

There was growing concern, fueled by a serious music press and a not-so-serious tabloid contingent, that at the ripe old age of twenty-three, Adele had possibly done permanent damage to her voice. It seemed like a classic Greek tragedy, done up pop-music style, was in the making.

If Adele was losing sleep over the seemingly growing problem, she was not letting on, preferring instead to bask in the glory of *21*'s worldwide success.

Adele attended a best friend's wedding in October and did not think twice about honoring the happy couple as only she could. She began to sing . . .

Adele instantly knew something was wrong.

It was later determined that a polyp had formed on her vocal cords and that surgery would be necessary—not the words anybody who lives and dies by their voice wants to hear. At least outwardly, Adele remained calm. She found the best medical minds in the business to diagnose her problem and to suggest a cure. Surgery was performed in early November. The surgery was a success. Whether or not she would ever sing again was still in question.

And how do we know all this? Because in Adele's world, there are no secrets.

Be it her weight, her love life or lack of same, her smoking, her drinking . . . you ask it and Adele will answer it. She has been fond of saying that "she loves food and hates exercise." When a French media outlet broke the news that

Adele had reportedly made a sex tape, she laughingly denied the allegation and promptly sued for damages. She freely discusses ex-loves but has refused to name them, preferring to relegate them to a much-deserved past that she might only bring up for inspiration. She sometimes drank to excess and has been willing to share the gory details. Dr. Phil would not have to probe too hard to discover Adele's insecurities; she would be only too happy to volunteer them, because the word "lie" is simply not in her vocabulary.

It is an understatement to say that Adele was born telling the truth—on the mean streets of Tottenham.

Adele is a no-nonsense by-product of a rough-and-tumble, working-class, high-unemployment, high-crime area of England, a world where fakes and phonies are simply not tolerated. She learned early on not to dance around reality—a reality that is in her songs, her heart, and in her life.

Which, if you examine Adele closely, are one and the same. It has not been uncommon for Adele to break down while singing a song that reflects a very real hurt, a very real triumph, or an emotional breakthrough of mammoth proportions. Merely talking about her songs and the emotions they bring has often caused Adele to tear up during press interviews.

You can't fake that kind of involvement in music, and it goes without saying that Adele does not have a fake bone in her body. It's believable when Adele says that she always wanted to be a singer, but that she is amazed and sometimes uneasy with being in the eye of the storm that stardom entails. Truth is her mantra.

She's a reporter's delight and a publicist's constant challenge. She has always been free and easy with the notion that major inspiration for her first two albums had been love affairs gone wrong and was more than willing to dissect them for the public. When most entertainers pull in their horns and go into a shell at the first sign of trouble or controversy, Adele seems to welcome and, yes, relish those interested in her life and world.

Which is why Adele, in just a handful of years, has become the new darling of the international press. She has forced the jaded media to take a different approach. Adele is not one of the normal run of pampered, vacuous, and often talent-challenged cartoon figures that normally grace the covers of *Vogue, Rolling Stone,* and *People* in varying states of dress and undress. Model-thin sexuality is not her stock-in-trade.

Her rags-to-riches story being paraded across the newsstands and Web sites of the world comes across as the closest thing to normal the pop music scene has seen in ages. Adele has been presented as every woman, the one we should all root for and, by degrees, emulate. She is the one we can see ourselves hanging with, sharing a drink and some gossip and acting the fool on occasion. In other words . . . human.

And her humanity is reflected in her values.

She has been steadfast in her refusal to become a brand and has refused big-money endorsement deals. For the longest time, she refused to do large arenas and outdoor festivals before the economics of the business forced her to modify that stance. With success has come untold riches, but she remains unfazed at the prospect of millions.

"I share my money with my friends and family," she told

The Sun. "I bought my mother a used car, and I got a dog and some handbags. I was happy when I didn't have money, and I would be happy if I didn't have it again."

Calling Adele a modern-day Eliza Doolittle is as close to being spot-on as one could get.

And it certainly has not hurt her cause that, along with these virtues, she is also very talented.

When Adele performs, it's a very simple concept. No outlandish, revealing costumes. Adele has constantly had a good laugh at the notion being on stage and showing her tits, something she would never do. No lavish stage shows that require monster trucks to haul around. Some subtle, well-placed lights, a piano, a guitar, a thoughtful and subtle backing band—all focused on the star of the show: Adele's voice and her songs.

And when she sings, there's a fragility and sincerity to it all. It has become quickly apparent in her short run up the ladder of success that Adele, much like her idol Etta James, is in it for the long haul. She admits to admiration for the late Amy Winehouse and, in her most vulnerable moments, there is that haunting similarity. But there is one defining difference.

Nobody is more aware of Adele and her talent than XL Recordings founder Richard Russell. His company took the financial and other risks when they signed the then-unknown on the strength of a three-song demo. He remains steadfast in the notion that Adele has single-handedly turned the music industry on its ear at a time when it was, to many observers, hanging on by its fingertips.

"The whole message with Adele is that it's just music," he

told *The Guardian*. "There are no gimmicks and no selling of sexuality. It's nothing else but the music."

Adele believes in what she is doing far too much to flame out. If the fates allow, she's a singer who will be around for a while.

Which was why, well into November and the recovery period that might determine whether or not she would ever sing again, the press were a fair constant in her world. Adele let us in on the recovery process, her hopes for the future, her seeming lack of fear, and of course, the most recent love of her life, whom she has enthused over, and who has been a major element in her rounding into emotional shape post-surgery.

The press reported Adele was romantically involved. She was profane and attacking when she found out that her long-estranged father had sold his story to the tabloids and had essentially put to rest any possibility of reconciliation.

And what it all meant in Adele's world was a fairly simple equation: Her music. Her passions. Her life. Her way.

An early Christmas present came with the announcement that Adele was all over the nominations for the 2012 Grammy Awards that would take place in February. It was almost a given that, of her six nominations for *21*, Adele would walk off with most if not all of them.

What was more of a dramatic aside was Adele's plan to come out of her medically imposed exile from performing on that night and sing for the first time since the operation. Could she pull it off or would the Grammys be an ironic finale to a meteoric rise?

It would either be the beginning or the end. And Adele would not have it any other way.

ADELE

ONLY THE BEGINNING

Adele loves her mother. Always has. Always will.
"You don't realize how important your parents are until you've spent a lot of time away from them," she was quoted on the Web site Great Personalities. "My mother and I have always been friends but we're tighter than ever now. We can talk about anything and not just in a mother-daughter way."

But as a *Vogue* journalist discovered during a 2011 interview, her feelings toward her father are a whole other matter: "If I ever see him, I will spit in his face."

And a journalist for *Rolling Stone* received a similar response when the question of her father was broached: "He has no fucking right to talk about me."

Adele's responses were toward questions about her father's reemergence in the pages of *The Sun* newspaper, telling about those early days with Adele and her mother. In Adele's view, he added insult to injury by supplying the paper with rarely seen photos of her as a child. She considered it an intrusion and a betrayal of the highest order, made all the more evil by the fact that he was paid quite handsomely for the interview and photos. For Adele, the act was the final nail in the coffin of an already tenuous relationship, one that just a year previous was showing signs of a reconciliation.

"I don't know what a dad is supposed to do because I never had one," she said in a *MusicLife* story. "I'm sure I will see him again. I think we can be friends. I don't need him to be a dad now."

But it was not meant to be.

Adele is not the first superstar talent to be estranged from a parent. In fact, it comes as a surprise when a reigning celebrity has come from a happy, intact, and functional family. But the obvious anger in Adele's thoughts when it comes to dealing with the biological dad she rarely saw and now does not see at all, is palpable.

Armchair psychiatrists have been quick to blame the lion's share of Adele's much-publicized relationship difficulties on the fact that she essentially grew up without a father figure. Adele has never addressed the impact not having a father may have had. But one thing is certain . . .

. . . Adele has been adamant in her estrangement from Mark Evans and, indirectly, keeping her father at arm's length has only served to cloud the details of how her parents met and how she came to be. She has only spoken about that element of her history when pressed, and then we've only gotten the broad strokes. Her parents met quite young. Adele's mother became pregnant. They never married, and her father moved out when Adele was a toddler. There were always the tabloid allegations; Evans was a notorious womanizer and an alcoholic according to the more colorful media outlets.

Of the latter, Evans, in a far-reaching interview with *The Sun*, admitted as much. But until Adele decides to completely chronicle her history or her mother decides to talk, there is largely only Evans' recounting of those early days to rely on.

Mark Evans was raised in the Welsh seaside town of Penarth. By all accounts, he was cut from simple, working-man stock and maintained a likable, salt-of-the-earth personality. He was once described in one of Adele's charitable moments as "The big Welsh guy who works on the ships." His looks: rugged yet youthful. Chances are, if you threw a rock in Wales in the late '70s and early '80s, hitting a Mark Evans type would not be difficult.

He was straightforward in his outlook, basic in his attitude, and it goes without saying that he was not a creative bloke and certainly not musically inclined.

He would seem an odd choice for Penny Adkins.

Penny was born in Tottenham, an equally working-class enclave of North London, to grocer John Adkins and his wife, Doreen. The city of Tottenham had an illustrious history of turning out inventors, statesmen, and no shortage of entertainers that included Dave Clark (of Dave Clark Five music fame), musician Lemar Obika, and actors Ron Moody and Shani Wallace. There was a consensus that being from Tottenham was something special and a legitimate source of pride. So much so that, following the 2012 Grammy Awards, Adele stated proudly in a *Sun* feature, "I'm not a fake Tottenham girl. I was born there."

But the years and the economy had not been kind to the town of Tottenham. The city of Tottenham was a sturdy blue-collar place that, with the years, had evolved into a decidedly bleak low-income enclave whose population had become used to hard times, poverty, and little in the way of a future. If you were from Tottenham, you hoped for the best. And the best was usually avoiding jail, death, or unplanned parenthood.

Penny had grown up to be the exception to the rule.

Penny Adkins was an attractive, creative, and quite adventurous young woman, heavily into the arts and, at age eighteen, an art student with a bright future in front of her. She was clearheaded when it came to avoiding the pitfalls of being a teen. Her parents encouraged her to be something special. Penny was enamored of music but had not seemed inclined to pursue it. The young girl was looked upon by those who knew her as a "Great White Hope," somebody who was on the verge of overcoming the odds and leaving Tottenham behind for something better.

In keeping with the Adkins family tradition, Penny, at eighteen, was already out of her parents' home and living an independent life. In a March 2011 interview with *The Sun*, Doreen Adkins recalled, "We threw Adele's mum out when she was eighteen. That's what we did with all the kids. They had to make their own way in life."

Mark and Penny met in 1987 in a London pub. They hit it off immediately. Penny has never been candid in assessing what she liked about Adele's future father, but in *The Sun* interview, Mark was intent in what made his heart skip a beat.

"Penny was amazing," he said. "She was a gorgeous-looking woman with real presence. She was intelligent, creative, and she knew how to make you laugh."

It was the classic case of opposites attracting.

The relationship between the couple developed at lightning speed. The impression from those who must have looked back on the couple's courtship was that neither of them was looking at it as being long lasting and serious. They became intimate almost immediately. In a matter of months, Penny broke the news to her parents that she was pregnant with Evans' child. Evans' parents were reportedly extremely upset that their son had gotten a young teenager pregnant. On the other hand, Penny's mother, Doreen, told *The Sun*, "I wasn't that shocked when she got pregnant."

"She fell pregnant with me when she would have been applying for uni (university)," Adele recalled in a conversation with *The Observer*. "But she chose to have me instead. She never, ever reminds me of that. I try to remember it."

Penny's parents were equally upset at the news. But this sort of thing happened with regularity in Tottenham, and all that was left was for them to put the best possible face on the situation. Penny's parents remained optimistic and supportive of the union—easily more so than Penny.

For while Mark stated in the *Daily Mail* interview that he was ready to step up and do the right thing, Penny, perhaps sensing the fragility of their relationship, reportedly chose cohabitation with Mark over a legal marriage on the grounds that they were both too young to commit to each other in that way.

Mark and Penny moved into a house two blocks away from Penny's parents. Mark found employment as a plumber while Penny gave up all prospects of school and career to be a stay-at-home mother-in-waiting.

The ensuing months must have been an emotional roller coaster for the couple. Penny's heart was obviously not in the relationship, and she saw few prospects for the future. It might have also been a case of realizing that any hope for a creative life in the arts was going by the wayside. This would have been in stark contrast to Mark's determination to make the relationship work. It would not have been the best circumstances for bringing a child into the world.

Adele Laurie Blue Adkins was born on May 5, 1988.

The arrival of the newborn did little to salve the erratic nature of Mark and Penny's relationship. By his own estimation, Mark was very young and wild and, once the novelty of a child wore off, he would be a regular at the local pubs, preferring the company of his friends and a pint to that of Penny and Adele.

However, in the *Sun* interview, Evans did relate some warm father and daughter moments in which he may well have given his daughter a subconscious sense of musical influences that would shape her life and career.

"I'd lie on the sofa, all night, cradling Adele in my arms and listening to my favorite music . . . Ella Fitzgerald, Louis Armstrong, Bob Dylan, and Nina Simone. Night after night I would play those records and I am certain that is what shaped Adele's music."

As the years passed, Penny could sense that the relationship had run its course. When Adele was three years old, Mark left the house and never came back.

Penny did little to stop him from leaving.

The split between Penny and Mark was surprisingly amicable. Evans returned to Wales where he continued to drink heavily after the deaths of his father and a close friend. He became involved in other relationships and fathered another child. Money was always tight, but Evans would send Penny some money when he could.

For a time, Adele was still a part of his life. There would be sporadic visits by Penny and Adele to Wales over the next couple of years. Evans would marvel at how his daughter had gravitated toward music. He related in the *Sun* interview that Adele had come to visit around the time she turned four and brought along a used acoustic guitar her mother had picked up in a charity shop. "She told me that she was teaching herself to play by listening to blues records on an old record player and trying to make the same noises."

Sadly, the visits became less and less frequent as Evans

fell victim to alcoholism, and by the time Adele had turned seven, Evans was essentially out of her life.

Penny and Adele had taken up residence in a cramped Tottenham flat in a less-than-ideal part of the city. But Penny proved resourceful and determined to make the best of life as a single mother and to provide for her infant daughter. Her enterprising spirit at jobs such as masseuse, furniture maker, and office administrator carved out a less-than-lavish but comfortable existence.

"She always had to do things, whether she wanted to or not, to get money to bring me up," Adele told *The Scotsman*.

Owing to the intricacies of the British subsidized housing system, Penny and Adele moved with regularity to various low-income flats. It was a life that would have easily beaten down lesser souls.

But Adele, who early on began to refer to her mother as "hippie mum" because of her artistic nature, has often said that the nomadic lifestyle was more of an ongoing adventure than an ordeal born of poverty, and often credits her mother with making even the most dire circumstances fun.

"I never had an issue of being comfortable in my own skin," she explained during a segment of the television show *CBS This Morning*. "That came from my mum."

Adele had also acknowledged that her mother would regularly tell her that she should do what she felt was best for her and not for others.

Adele's early years were shaped by a real sense of family in and around Tottenham. She often spoke of aunts she would stay with when her mother was at work and, of course, there were Penny's parents, grandparents, cousins, and siblings at all hours of the day and night. With an estimated thirty-three family members about, Adele was never alone. Sometimes, she recalled in a *Guardian* interview, she relished the moments when she was.

"I'd go and see them (the family) and they were always arguing and hating to share. Then I would go back to my tidy room and my unbroken toys. I had the best of both worlds."

Even in the most chaotic family moments, she would remember that there always seemed to be music playing. Oftentimes it would be the radio blaring out the pop hits of the day. Sometimes it would be the older family members' classical and jazz records. There would always be something to listen to.

But she would often insist that the best times were when she and her mother were alone; "Thick as thieves," she recalled.

It was inevitable that Penny and Adele would have their dustups over the young girl's acting out or moments of misbehavior. Adele recalled in *Out* magazine that she would respond to those disagreements with pencil and paper.

"Being an only child, I was never very good at saying how I felt about things. So from about age five, I would always write my apology out if I did something wrong and give it to her. Over the years there must have been hundreds of notes."

Like most children, Adele went through her fantasy phase where she imagined herself in grown-up occupations. When Adele's grandfather died, the then ten-year-old Adele advanced the notion that she would be a heart surgeon. "I think I wanted to be a heart surgeon," she told *State Magazine*. "I wanted to be able to help people and fix people."

When a very young Adele announced that her ambition was to grow up and be, by turns, a mum, a weather girl, or a ballet dancer, Penny would never dismiss these childish notions out of hand but would be diligent in gently pointing her daughter in a far more ambitious, logical direction.

"My mother was the most encouraging person," Adele told a *Telegraph* journalist. "She was always telling me to explore and to not just stick with one thing."

Adele took the encouragement to heart and, without the least amount of direction, quite naturally gravitated toward the notion of voices and, by association, singing and music. How voices sounded and changed became an obsession. So did the way singers sounded.

Music became a constant in the flat: blues, jazz, soul, and late '80s pop and new wave. Penny was young enough to be hip when it came to the music of the day and so it was not unusual for her to extol the virtues of 10,000 Maniacs and Bob Dylan, Janis Joplin, and Jeff Buckley. However, Adele always seemed to gravitate toward love songs, as she explained to *The Sun*.

"I always loved the ones about horrible relationships. Those were the ones you could relate to and that always made you cry."

And the very first song that made her shed tears was "Troy" by Sinéad O'Connor. It made such a strong impression that, years later, Adele would consider doing a cover of the song. She would later relent on the grounds that she did not think she could do it justice.

Although not musically inclined beyond pure enjoyment, Adele would often showcase an intuitive/sensitive side when it came to a song that she sensed meant something deeper. Adele would often be found off in a corner, reading the sleeve notes and lyric sheets that accompanied her favorite albums and daydreaming about when she was going to feel the things those songs talked about.

The always progressive-thinking Penny saw fit to feed Adele's interest in music by taking the then three-year-old to her first concert, a show by the group The Cure. It is a safe assumption that Adele's first concert experience was a largely nonsensical blur of sights and sounds. But the experience became an important part of her early psyche.

The Cure would be Adele's first big influence. The group's intensity, emotion, and pure soulfulness struck a chord in the young child's flowering musical influences. And she would continue to experience the group through their records non-stop in her early childhood years.

"The Cure was the sound track to my life until I was nine," Adele said in an interview with *The Scotsman*.

Their music would remain a constant even after she sought out new musical heroes, and recently, Adele paid homage to that all-important element of her being by covering The Cure's signature song, "Lovesong."

Ever the liberal parent, Penny also stretched some rules by allowing Adele, at age four, a regular pass on a good night's sleep so she could stay up late and watch the popular music show, *Later . . . with Jools Holland,* a UK tradition which show-cased the top musical stars of the day as well as the occasional newcomer. Even at four, Adele would be fascinated by the notion of pop stars and the attention they received. Adele looked at the music heroes of the day as only a child would. It was a neat fantasy to watch and dream about. But Adele at age four could hardly be accused of taking a life in music seriously.

It would remain for pop music's flavor of the moment, Spice Girls, to finally point Adele on a musical path. Adele came upon the group at age six. They were all over the radio for a time; she would get the records and catch every opportunity to see the group perform on television. Everything about the group fascinated her: the songs, the singing, the over-the-top pop personalities. She would readily admit to the obsession in an interview with *Ahlan! Live*.

"I was obsessed with them! I wrote a blog about them at one point. I went to see them at Wembley Arena and Earls Court back in the day."

And looking back, Adele makes no bones about the fact that they influenced her life.

"The Spice Girls made me what I am today," she told the Minneapolis *StarTribune*. "I knew it was kind of cheesy but that was my generation."

And she found a willing accomplice to her Spice Girls obsession in her mother. Adele had found her muse in Spice Girls and, to a slightly lesser degree, pop singer Gabrielle, and even as a young child, she had become fairly adept at mimicking the singers' voices.

"I would be singing the song 'Dreams' by Gabrielle," she told *Ahlan! Live*, "and my mum would hear me and say 'you sound like a twenty-year-old.'"

Penny was more than willing to play along and would

regularly invite family and friends over to their flat for mini-concerts.

"My mum's quite arty," she related to *The Independent* and countless other outlets as part of a story Adele seemingly never gets tired of telling. "She'd get all these lamps and shine them up to make one big spotlight."

Those privy to Adele's earliest performances have indicated that the youngster definitely had a gift for impersonation, but that it still played out as a game with little if any serious intent.

Adele began her schooling in Tottenham. The reality was that Tottenham was economically segregated and largely populated by African and Caribbean immigrants. The crime rate was high. The unemployment rate was higher. Tottenham was recognized as one of the UK's most hopeless outposts.

From the outset, formal education and Adele seemed an oil-and-water mix. By all accounts, the young child was bright and inquisitive. And like most young children, Adele could be easily distracted if what was being taught did not interest her. She could be rambunctious when the mood struck her.

So it was not surprising that even at a young age Adele's free-spirited nature ran afoul of teachers who had little on their agendas but to teach the basics that would ensure a low-paying, dead-end, and decidedly uncreative life.

"Growing up, I had to bear the brunt of negative attitudes from authority figures, like teachers, who led me to believe that success was unrealistic," she said. "My response to that was to escape into a world of fantasy because I was not very good academically."

Adele was one of only a handful of white students in the largely black school. At first it was difficult not to notice that she stood out, but after a while she stopped noticing the difference. Never a brilliant student, Adele nevertheless managed to get by academically, fit in with her classmates, and make friends easily.

But it was never a perfect fit. Adele would lapse into periods of being standoffish and sullen, and there was no getting around the fact that Adele was a big girl, and kids would sometimes be cruel when it came to issues of weight and body image. But with her mother's support, Adele would get through the rough times relatively unscathed.

Adele and her mother relocated to Brixton when she was nine. Much like Tottenham, Brixton was a rough-and-tumble, blue-collar, multiracial town. Prospects, economically and otherwise, were limited, although Brixton had turned out a more-than-expected collection of famous residents that included former British Prime Minister John Major and rock stars David Bowie, and Mick Jones and Paul Simonon of The Clash.

School was still a necessary evil for Adele, but she continued to slowly but surely see music as more than a passing fancy. Adele continued to be fond of the guitar and had developed basic skills on clarinet and bass. Adele's voice was still a raw instrument but was showing surprising pitch and control for an untrained child. It was the rare moment when Adele could not be heard singing her favorite songs while in the shower or walking down the street.

"My first public singing experience was at a school show at age eleven," she explained to *Ahlan! Live*. "My mum had made me an eye patch with sequins on it to wear so I would look like Gabrielle. I liked the patch so much that I would continue to wear it to school and I would get in trouble for it."

Experiences like this were playing to Adele's ego and her growing need to be the center of attention. But even as she was accepting applause for her performances, singing was still nothing more than fun and games.

Adele and her musically inclined friends would regularly get together for impromptu song sessions, and the songs that Adele would belt out with vigor were the pop hits of the day, songs like "Independent Woman, Part 1" and "Survivor" by Destiny's Child. During these street and schoolyard sessions, Adele would mug and pose and, along with her friends, laugh up a storm. Nobody was taking it seriously. Not even Adele.

While her tastes were largely running to the pop of the moment, Adele's mother saw to it that her daughter received a healthy dose of rock, soul, rhythm & blues, and mild hip-hop. Music by Mary J. Blige, Alicia Keyes, and Lauryn Hill became the sound track around the Brixton flat. When her mother developed a crush on Jeff Buckley, that's all Adele heard. R.E.M., Dylan, and Janis Joplin continued as major items on what would become a musical mix that, according to a *Rolling Stone* assessment, became a "life-defining" time for the youngster.

Adele would often acknowledge that, like most young people, she was, by degrees, tolerant, impatient, and dismissive with her mother's musical choices growing up, but that she eventually came around to appreciate her mother's esoteric choices. And that what she was hearing was "amazing."

It would soon be a life-defining time for Adele's mother. After a number of years alone, Penny fell in love and eventually married. Adele was quite happy for her mother and had a good feeling about the new man in her mother's life. By the time Adele turned eleven, the family was off to another residence. . . .

And a new adventure.

3.

THE MICROPHONE

West Norwood, in the south of London, was considered a step up from Penny and Adele's previous neighborhoods. Largely residential, and more than a touch suburban, the town, in the borough of Lambeth, had libraries, theaters, and more than its share of middle-class trappings. Like every other place Adele had lived, West Norwood had a history of an eclectic mix of famous residents. Sir John Scarlett, the former head of the British intelligence unit MI6, called West Norwood home, as have singers Maxi Jazz and Des'ree.

But Penny and her husband were still on the downside. Their job situations remained spotty and low paying. They could not afford much but managed to get by. Their home in West Norwood was a run-down flat over the This That & The Other retail store on the less-than-stellar West Norwood High Street. As always, poverty took a back burner to the fantasy of real life and the continued determination of Penny to nourish her daughter's growing musical aspirations.

Penny managed to scrape together enough money to get Adele some semblance of formal music lessons and, most nights, would hurry home from work and rush her to her music classes, where she was beginning to learn the fundamentals of guitar and piano. The instruction she was receiving was basic, but Adele remained fairly attentive, since the notion of learning and playing music and how it fit into her fantasy world was now firmly planted in her life plan.

Saturday mornings would also be part and parcel of Adele's on-the-job education in all things pop.

On those mornings when Adele could wake up early enough, she would take the tube to the heart of London and stand in line in hopes of being selected as part of the live audience for the TV music show *CountDown: United Kingdom*, which featured live performances, interviews with the top names of the day, and performance videos.

By age eleven, singing was very much an element of Adele's world. Singing professionally was only in her fantasies, but as an informal, very amateur exercise, it had become a part of her everyday life—except when it came to school. The primary school she was attending in West Norwood was strictly by the book, and Adele soon found out that wanting to sing would not be encouraged.

"The teacher was a bit rubbish," Adele recalled in an interview with *The Independent*. "They gave me a really hard time. They would try to bribe me, saying that if I wanted to sing, I would first have to play clarinet."

Adele was openly defiant. Her already spotty attendance

record became even worse, with truancies and late arrivals continuing to pile up. Never academically inclined to begin with, her grades began to suffer. While her mother continued to be supportive, Penny must have feared that her daughter would end up settling for much less in life. But there was also an upside to the daily ordeal that formal education had turned into.

Adele had fallen in with a fairly hip crowd of classmates by the time she had reached secondary school, and through them, she was introduced to a wide array of modern pop influences that she had never considered. Destiny's Child, Faith Evans, and P. Diddy became regulars on her turntable and, as it turned out, during impromptu jam sessions on the streets and stoops of West Norwood.

"Getting into that kind of music was a way to meet kids on a social level," she said in her official Web site biography. "I met all the R&B kids and we would all get together on the playground and sing."

But while she worked hard at being musically hip around her friends, at night, alone in her room, she would secretly revert to pop favorites and the stylings of Spice Girls and Celine Dion.

Adele continued to explore other forms of music and, at age thirteen, had what she considers her defining moment when she saw Pink live in concert.

"I remember seeing Pink at the Brixton Academy," she related in a conversation with Spinner. "It was the time of the *Missundaztood* record. I had never heard, being in the room, someone sing like that live. I remember sort of feeling like I was in a wind tunnel, her voice just hitting me. Before that I had been into the Spice Girls, who obviously did not know how to sing, and now I know that. But Pink that night was just incredible."

Around this time, Adele, more as a fashion statement and defiant stance than any serious musical statement, embraced the hard-core metal genre, dressing in what passed for hard-core couture and spending hours at the local record shop, looking only halfheartedly through the latest offerings by Korn and Slipknot and sensing that, like her previous infatuations, this too would pass.

"I was just pretending that I liked hard-core rock like Korn and Slipknot to be cool," she confessed to *The Telegraph*. "I actually hated it. That stuff scared me."

As she looked through the shelves, she eventually wandered down to the basement of the shop that was off-limits to just about anybody who could not remember the 1940s. But Adele began poking around the shelves and spotted an album by blues/jazz legend Etta James staring back at her. Adele eyed the picture of James a moment and then bought the disc—not so much to listen to the music as to show her hairdresser a hairstyle she was interested in trying.

"I saw the most stunning woman I had ever seen in my life," recalled the singer in a conversation with National Public Radio. "She had this beehive weave and these catty eyes and this seductive figure and this look on her face like 'Don't mess with me.'"

As the store was having a two-for-ten-dollars sale on older titles, she also decided that an Ella Fitzgerald cover looked interesting and took that home as well.

Eventually Adele got around to actually playing the Etta

James CD, found a lot in the music she admired and, most important, decided that that was the kind of singing she should be doing.

"She went right through me," Adele told National Public Radio. "It was the first time I had ever been so moved by someone's voice. It was like she was singing a song that was written for me."

Pressing her luck, Adele played the Ella Fitzgerald collection and, as in James, found a music out of her time that was speaking to her. She continued her musical exploration, and other grand ladies of blues and old soul were soon making inroads into Adele's world. While her friends scoffed at Adele's latest choices, the teen knew in her gut that this kind of music was pointing her in the right direction.

Word began to spread among Adele's school chums about her growing interest in "their parents' kind of music" and through them, their parents would often contribute to Adele's musical education in the classics.

"I was over at my friend Alicia's house one day and I remember her mom playing a Billie Holiday record, 'God Bless the Child,'" she told *HITS* magazine. "It was unlike anything I had ever heard. I loved the passion in it and it was all about the voice. I believed her, and there are not many artists that I believe."

Singing was a constant at this point. In the shower, in the car, while the family was at dinner. It had become so ingrained that, at one point, Penny enthusiastically suggested that her daughter audition for the British forerunner of *American Idol*, the show *PopStars*. Adele declined the suggestion.

"I just wasn't convinced doing a show like that was a

good idea," she told *Pollstar*. "You know, you get these parents and they're like, 'She's the next Whitney,' and then she sings and it's awful."

At age thirteen, Adele was not above having a bit of a lark when she appeared in the direct to DVD movie *Ushi Says: Hi!*. In this comedy about an inept celebrity interviewer, Adele joined such B-list celebrities as Donny Osmond and La Toya Jackson as celebrity interview subjects. According to all reports, Adele acquited herself quite well in this small role. But an acting career was not something that seemed interesting to Adele.

A career in music seemed to be the logical alternative to her abject failure and disinterest in school. Adele had grown to have little patience with her classmates, whom she considered rude, crude, and destined for a life of poverty and crime. She was failing all her classes. She had no interest in what formal education had to offer and was admittedly in the dark about anything that did not entail singing.

The final push came in 2003 when the then fourteen-year-old Adele was complimented after one of her impromptu home shows by a friend of her stepfather. This acquaintance offered to record Adele singing the Blondie hit "Heart Of Glass" as an informal test so the youngster could get an idea of how her voice sounded.

Adele recalled in an AceShowbiz story, "As soon as I got the microphone in my hand, I realized I wanted to do this. Most people don't like the way their voice sounds when it is recorded. I was just so excited by the whole thing that I wasn't bothered what I sounded like."

Adele did not get much of an argument from her mother

when she announced that she had had enough of formal education and was going off to be a singer. Adele did acknowledge the fact that some education in the finer points of singing would be necessary. Initially she thought the famed Sylvia Young Theater School would be the way to go, seeing as how her idol Baby Spice had attended that school. But that direction was dashed because her mother could not afford the hefty tuition, and Adele's negative impression of Sylvia Young students as arrogant, stupid, and not very talented would tip the scales.

The BRIT School, a Performing Arts and Technology School, was a whole other story. Since its inception in 1991, The BRIT School has been a largely free-form high school similar to the one in the movie *Fame*. The institution offers talented students the opportunity to learn everything they need to know about their creative goals and allows room for self-expression and experimentation. The school had quietly garnered a reputation by graduating a number of future professionals in the areas of music and theater. No superstars to speak of. No storied alumni and, most certainly, no pop music icons. The music industry at large was conspicuous by its lack of interest in the school's regularly scheduled performances.

BRIT seemed the ideal choice for a number of reasons: It was free. She could focus entirely on music and song. And, most importantly, she was far away from the death grip formal education had been.

"I went there simply because I hated my first high school," she told *HITS*. "There were no aspirations and no encouragement there for anything other than getting to the end and getting pregnant. The state schools I went to were really rough."

Adele's bleak memories of her last formal education were balanced out by the recollections of deputy headteacher Dominic Bergin at Chestnut Grove School, the last school Adele attended before applying to BRIT. In a *Guardian* interview, he remembered Adele as being a diligent student.

"Adele was just a normal school girl," he recalled. "She was a very nice girl, although I did remember that she dressed a bit grungy. My wife, Catherine, used to teach her English and said she was kind, hardworking, motivated, and academically very able."

While considering BRIT, Adele would also discover that after being below the radar, The BRIT School was becoming hip to the modern pop world.

A new crop of students were entering the school with a larger worldview in mind. Adele would occasionally brush shoulders with Amy Winehouse as she wandered through the halls between the music and theater departments. And she would find much in common with fellow newcomers and future hit-makers Jessie J, Leona Lewis, and Kate Nash.

Adele auditioned for the BRIT program and was accepted. She recalled in *CBS This Morning* that she filled out a massive application and then it came down to a final meeting with school music director Liz Perry. When they saw talent in the audition, things boiled down to one simple question: "She asked me why they should let me in. I said, 'Because I'm creative.'"

Even after being accepted, Adele was still expressing doubt and insecurities about finally taking steps toward a professional life. "At that point, I never thought my being a professional singer was going to happen," she said in a Free

Library Web site interview. "So (part of me) felt that it was a waste of time pursuing something that, most likely, was not going to happen. Then there was a part of me that thought it was simply a stage school and that I could do what I needed to do on my own."

However Adele was street smart enough to realize that the alternative to BRIT was a dead-end life, as she explained in an interview with *News of the World*. "I'd hate to think where I would have ended up if I hadn't gone to the BRIT school. It's quite inspiring to be around seven hundred kids who want to do something rather than being around seven hundred kids who just want to get pregnant so they can get their own flat."

Once she got over her initial bout of nerves, Adele soon found herself in the middle of the creative whirlwind that was BRIT. It was not uncommon for Adele to be walking down the hallway and run headlong into a group of kids doing dance routines. Budding mimes would regularly practice their trade in a stairwell, dancers would be practicing ballet moves in the hallways, and spontaneous singing contests would spring up just about anywhere on the BRIT campus during the course of the day.

Adele's school chum Jessie J told The Associated Press about the freewheeling times at The BRIT School. "Adele was in music and I was in musical theater. We used to jam at lunchtime. Someone would play guitar and we would both sing."

The spontaneity of it all was not lost on Adele.

"It was inspiring to be around a bunch of kids who were trying to be something," she said in a Free Library interview. "Sometimes I just wanted to get up and leave because when you are trying to be creative, it can get quite frustrating at times."

Especially when Adele's heart, even at that late day, was not totally into it. "I never deliberately pursued being a singer," she confessed to The MIX. "I was studying music just because I had so much energy and I wanted to channel it. Singing was the only thing I liked to do and it seemed that was the only thing that people seemed pleased to teach me."

Inwardly, Adele had the passion. But as she wandered through her days at BRIT, she would often come across as aloof and withdrawn amid the creative energy crackling at BRIT. But that Adele had that "something" was something that her classmates picked up on.

Allan Rose was at The BRIT School the same time as Adele and, as described in an AceShowbiz story, had a front row seat as the future star came of age.

"It was clear that she was going to be a star. Some people were that step above everyone else and Adele was one of them. She was bubbly, fun, outgoing, and popular in school."

Former classmate and current Adele guitarist Ben Thomas recalled in a *Rolling Stone* interview that Adele's drive to succeed was often in question. "There were some people at school who really pushed hard. You could tell they really wanted it. Adele never really had that."

But Thomas was quick to acknowledge that "she was a great performer and everyone would be completely silent and in awe when she performed."

Midway through her tenure at BRIT, Adele was beginning to round into shape as a performer. She would agree with the slightest compliment and had a growing confidence in her own talents. It would remain for a family vacation to America when Adele was fifteen to infuse an inner fantasy of pop stardom in the young girl.

"We were in New York and I remembered going into a massive Virgin music store," she told *PopCrush*. " I thought it would be amazing to one day have a record in a shop like that."

Adele returned to BRIT with a renewed sense of purpose. She knew what she wanted to be. Now if she could only figure out how to do it.

Adele eventually warmed to the idea of being in a totally free and expressive environment and, as she offered in an interview with *frankie* magazine, was suddenly as enthusiastic as she had ever been in her life.

"I saw that there were kids who were there on a Saturday morning, working because they loved it. I would literally jump out of bed in the morning, knowing that I would be going there. I'd never felt like that before."

But Adele was far from the perfect student. While she was a fairly diligent and attentive student in classes covering songwriting, singing, recording, and all manner of behind-the-scenes aspects of a singing career, she would relate in an interview with the *Daily Mail* that "My academic side went downhill and I played the class clown too often. But I loved the music lessons."

She would be the first to admit that she was fighting what The BRIT School was offering at every turn, even when it came to the music curriculum, according to an interview with the QMI Agency.

"I was quite stubborn," she related. "Sometimes I worked

hard and sometimes I didn't. But Liz Perry would always forgive me when I didn't and she was always patient with me. I was quite the stubborn teenager at The BRIT School. I only liked the music that I liked. I wasn't ready to be an eclectic, broad listener. Liz inspired me to that."

And her music instructor was forgiving when Adele was not at her best at BRIT. Because, as she explained to *MiND-FOOD*, with Adele there was always an upside. "Sometimes she worked very hard and sometimes not so hard. She was a bit of a chatterbox but she was always great fun. She had a strong will and a sense of purpose. Adele had the voice and sensibility to be able to pour her soul into her music."

But even when she was attentive to her studies, Adele would continue to have problems with being on time. It was not uncommon for her to oversleep and show up hours late for class, and on a couple of occasions, most notably a missed trip for a performance at a festival in Devon, she was on the cusp of being kicked out of school.

Rumors would spread that Adele, normally proper and subdued at school, was doing a bit of partying after hours. It was a speculation that Adele vehemently denied. Quite simply, she explained in *Rolling Stone*, "I just couldn't wake up."

However, when Adele was awake, her white-girl brand of soul and blues singing soon made her an urban legend on the BRIT campus. Either as part of a class exercise or whenever Adele felt like it, her singing inevitably brought the crowds, and those crowds were inevitably awed into silence by the passion in her voice. Despite all this, Adele has been known to occasionally downplay her star quality during her BRIT days, offering that she had been at odds with the school's approach to dissecting music and insisting that she had always been teaching herself.

"Brit didn't really shape my music," she told *State* magazine, "but it helped nurture my style of songwriting. I hadn't found my own voice but at Brit it just kind of appeared."

The youngster eventually found her songwriting inspiration after watching a documentary in which Marvin Gaye explained how he wrote songs even though he could not read music by writing the vocal parts and humming them to the guitarist. It was a revelation to Adele, who declared in *Vogue*, "It never really occurred to me to write my own songs and get away with it."

Given her current growing acclaim as the next Amy Winehouse, it was notable that midway through her BRIT career, Adele was seriously considering a career in the background as an A&R person who could help find and develop other talents. And she definitely had those qualifications. Adele had become quite the student of pop. She could instinctively tell what elements made a song good or bad. But uppermost, she was simply a fan of music, someone who had become quite savvy to the elements that went into making successful music and successful musicians even as she struggled with her own emerging performing personality.

The very nature of the BRIT curriculum kept Adele on a definite performing path. She had access to rehearsal rooms, free equipment, and the opportunity to listen to music all day. And what Adele did not get in the classroom, she more than made up for in 2004 when another aspiring singer, Shingai Shoniwa (who was beginning to gain notice with the up-and-coming band Noisettes), moved next door to

Adele's flat. The young singers struck up an immediate friend-ship centered around singing and songwriting.

Shoniwa related in a *Platforms Magazine* interview how the two met. "A lot of times people meet by listening through their apartment walls at what their neighbors are listening to. That's how Adele and I met. One day I heard her playing this shrieky saxophone through the walls. It turned out that we had some friends in common so that's how we got together."

Adele remembered their meeting somewhat the same.

"I used to hear her through the walls," Adele recalled in a 102.7 radio station Web site feature. "I used to go around and we'd jam and stuff like that. Just hearing her and her music made me want to be a writer and not just somebody who sang Destiny's Child songs."

It has been speculated that Adele had been playing around with songwriting on a very basic level throughout her later years at BRIT, but her perfectionist nature may have made her think that nothing she had written was wor-thy of being made public. But an argument with her mother in 2006, about where the then sixteen-year-old should attend university, changed all that.

At that time, Adele was favoring the University of London and the relative comfort of home and familiar surroundings. Penny strongly favored the University of Liverpool and let-ting her daughter be away from home to stand on her own two feet. After one particularly heated argument, Adele sat down with her guitar and wrote "Hometown Glory" in ten minutes.

"It was pretty simple," remembered Adele in a *Blues & Soul* magazine interview. "In her bittersweet and quite touching ode to London life, Adele addressed the issues of why she wanted to stay home. "It was just four chords on the guitar and pressing one string. I played it as a protest song to my mother. It basically said, 'This is why I'm staying.'"

2006 would continue to be an eventful year for Adele. She turned eighteen and graduated from BRIT in May. And then Adele fell in love for the very first time. First loves are typically challenging, but Adele's had the extra baggage of her lover being bisexual. The frustrations and the angst of this relationship were reflected in another of her early compositions, "Daydreamer."

"'Daydreamer' was about this boy I was in love with, like proper love," she said in her official Web site biography. "He was bi and I couldn't deal with that. All the things I wanted from my boyfriend, he was never going to be."

Another song written at the time, "My Same," was lyrically more wistful and longing but never strayed far from Adele's newfound muse: love captured, love lost.

And although she had developed a healthy relationship with her stepfather, more than one critic has offered that the lack of her biological father in her life may well have been a force in driving those early songs.

As part of her final-year requirements for graduation, Adele was instructed to create a demo tape of her songs. Thinking nothing more than a passing grade would come of the exercise, Adele dutifully recorded three of her own songs, "Hometown Glory," "Daydream," and "My Same." When a classmate, known only as Lyndon, suggested it might be fun to let him post the demo on Myspace, Adele did not think much of it. She had had a Web site of her own since 2003, but never thought much of the concept beyond being a tool of simple amusement. Adele had been recording demos throughout her stay at BRIT, but would typically turn them in to her instructor or pass them around to her friends and promptly forget about them.

But this time she agreed, more as a goof than anything else, to let her friend take her songs online. At that moment, she had no illusions about being discovered and becoming a star. She laughingly described the silliness of her situation to *The Telegraph*. "I was still in school. I wasn't doing any gigs. I wasn't on the circuit. I didn't believe you could get signed through Myspace.

"I figured the best that might come out of it was that I might get a job as an intern."

While still entertaining the dream of becoming a pop star, Adele would admit in a Behyped feature that she did not hold out high hopes. While others in the BRIT graduating class had already begun sending out demos in hopes of interesting a label, Adele's reality was still less ambitious, still self-defeating.

"I always knew I would be involved in music," she offered. "But I thought I'd be a receptionist or work in a shop and then, on my days off, I would go and play a little acoustic show for my family and friends. I didn't even bother to really seriously dream about being a singer. Everyone I knew had dreams and none of theirs had come true.

"So why the hell would mine?"

4

TICKET TO RIDE

A dele was about to find out just how powerful the Internet and social media could be.

When her admittedly primitive demo hit Myspace, the social networking service. When it came to discovering new music and artists, Myspace was at its zenith. It had not begun its decline to today's level, when contrived and obvious ways for questionable talent to get record deals seem the norm. Adele had caught the wave of legitimate exploration and discovery of budding talent, one that was made all the more possible in the UK after Lily Allen had parlayed her Myspace performance video into a recording contract. In the wake of such Internet successes as Allen and Justin Bieber, A&R people from record labels worldwide were anxiously scouring the Internet for the next big thing.

This was of no immediate concern to Adele who, following graduation, had been true to her bleak aspirations. By day she would work low-paying, dead-end jobs. She has never come clean as to what kinds of jobs they were, other than to indicate "I never had a proper job" in her blog. By night, she was a regular at the myriad of clubs in and around London, soaking up the atmosphere, enjoying music, and continuing to dream. But unbeknownst to her, the magic of the Internet was beginning to work wonders on Adele's primitive demo.

It was not long before an amazed Adele was getting worldwide attention from countless faceless fans who were drawn to her very real and passionate blend of pop and old soul. But while amazed, a leery Adele also questioned her Myspace success—around the time she had gathered 10,000 Internet friends.

Adele was old school through and through and, as such, had felt that a lot of dues-paying in endless clubs, honing any talent she felt she had in front of a live audience, was how it should be done. She had heard all the stories about immediate discovery via the Internet and wanted no part of it.

"I would hate to think I was a Myspace singer," she said in her Web site biography. "I've got no right to be that."

However, her Internet response only reinforced the notion that, in order to be a complete singer, she would have to begin playing in front of an audience. Adele had always been nervous about performing live, and never more so than when she began playing out midway through 2006.

It would be by choice that she went out alone, despite her attitude about pop music being about bands rather than solo performers. "When I started, I really didn't want to be in a band," she told the *Daily Mail*. "So I just got roped into the singer-songwriter thing."

Adele was about to test her talents in the harshest of arenas, the London club scene, which, after some admittedly lean years, was enjoying a resurgence.

Singer Jessie J described the prevailing London music scene when Adele arrived to *The Telegraph*. "When you're in a country that's smaller than Texas, you have to be yourself. You can't be fake or try to be like somebody else. In the UK, you're either yourself or you don't exist."

Adele entered a London music scene that was very much in transition. Less rigid and compartmentalized by genre than in years gone by, the current scene was very communally oriented, and musicians at different ends of the spectrum mixed easily and performed often in small clubs, offering a literal rainbow of musical colors. Musicians were friends rather than competitors. They reasoned that, when one musician or band was successful, they all were. Very artsy. Very '60s. It all seemed to be working.

Except for a disaster of a 2006 show in what Adele described to *Elle* as "a dinky little pub in East London."

"I thought I was going on at eight p.m., but it turned out that I wasn't on until two a.m. I had invited my friends and family and there was probably another three hundred people who had heard about me and who had come to watch. I got so drunk that, by the time I went on at two a.m., I forgot the words to my own songs and fell off the chair I was sitting on. It was the worst thing ever."

Adele beginning to play live was the direct result of her gregarious nature and an uncanny ability to strike up friendships out of the most surreal situations. She had made the acquaintance of singer-songwriter Jack Peñate at one of his gigs, and after a two-day pub crawl/food hunt through the Chelsea and Kings Road area, they were fast friends.

Penate told BBC Newsbeat that Adele and he "met in a very unglitzy, showy world and became friends through liking each other's music."

Jamie T came into Adele's world when he e-mailed her to compliment "Hometown Glory." Amos Lee? For Adele, this was hero worship come to life. She had been listening to the American-born singer for years.

These friendships had paved the way for Adele to enter the world of a very free-flowing group of up-and-coming eclectic London performers who saw Adele as somebody real and vital, which would result in Peñate, Jamie T, Raul Midón, Amos Lee, and Devendra Barnhart offering Adele slots whenever possible on their shows. Adele began getting her feet wet in a club scene that was a constant challenge. Lineups were often mismatched and Adele, armed with an acoustic guitar, her three songs, and powerful yet low-key vocals, could often be found sandwiched into a lineup that included raucous rappers, raging punks, and all manner and shades of new pop.

She would frequently be competing with loud and often intoxicated audience members, audience disinterest, and yes, the occasional fight. But what those privy to those early gigs also saw were nights when as few as ten club-goers, many of whom had no idea who Adele was, fell silent and sat enraptured as she weaved a quiet spell of emotional soul wrapped up in lyrics that told an age-old story of love lost and found.

Her set would usually consist of the three self-penned songs and the occasional nod to old soul favorites.

Adele fought back her earliest bouts of performance jitters by peppering her sets with between-song patter done up in her thick cockney accent. Tales of too much drink, how her songs came about and, to the inevitable cheers from the women in the audience, how a man had done her wrong. It was a style that the singer had stated had helped her out onstage and that, in some of those early shows, was instrumental in swaying indifferent club-goers over to her side.

Those privy to Adele's early twenty-minute support acts for the likes of Peñate were drawn to her voice and lyrics. There would be the occasional annoyance brought on by sloppy guitar playing. But at the end of the day, anyone who saw Adele in the early days came away impressed.

When not on stage, Adele was very much the social butterfly, chatting up club-goers before and after her sets, being a regular fan in the audience of friends when not performing, and making what she considered valuable contacts as well as friends. Years later she would explain how such a meeting resulted in meeting the person who would eventually become her full-time publicist.

Less than a month after graduating from BRIT, and after she began her initial forays into live performing, Adele's online demo began generating inquiries from record labels expressing degrees of interest. Adele was flattered but was in the dark about these e-mail advances.

Her knowledge of record labels began and ended with Virgin Records. But when the friend who had initially posted her demo excitedly told her that he was getting e-mails from the likes of Island Records and XL Recordings requesting a meeting, she was at a loss as to what to do. Her continued unease with the Internet had also made her somewhat skeptical of the offers.

"I'd never heard of those labels," she recalled in *Rolling Stone*. "I thought they were just some Internet perverts. So I didn't call them back."

Adele would later acknowledge that she was particularly leery of XL Recordings, imagining a deluded music wannabe sitting in his basement who would sign her to an ironclad ten-year deal and she would never be heard from again. "Besides," she told The MIX, "I was too busy organizing my eighteenth birthday to respond to any of them."

XL Recordings' A&R rep Nick Huggett was being particularly persistent in pursuing her, which he would explain in a Scenta article was a surprise even to him. "I didn't think I would ever sign anybody from the BRIT School for XL. But she had the most amazing voice I had ever come across."

Adele was still hesitant but, when her mother insisted she take a meeting and she discovered that XL was the home of such hip groups as The White Stripes and Radiohead, she felt that XL had to be legitimate.

Established in 1989, XL Recordings initially made its reputation as an independent label, supplying music for techno and rave fans. But as the company evolved into a legitimate indie, they honed their approach to signing and recording new artists with a worldwide audience in mind. They wanted artists who came to the table fully formed and with the ability to create real music, rather than prefab acts with little discernible talent or experience that would willingly be molded to any genre that made money.

Still there was the internal conflict. To Adele's way of thinking, XL's roster consisted of truly "out there" creative types who were actually making music, whereas Adele still saw herself as a non-inventive type simply singing mournful songs. Her insecurities resurfaced. She doubted that she had enough to say musically to justify the interest of a label.

Adele did not see what Nick Huggett saw.

However, she finally agreed to meet with XL. But not without bringing her longtime BRIT friend, and now occasional backing guitarist, Ben Thomas along . . . just in case.

"Ben is puny, he looks like a dwarf," Adele laughingly told *The Observer* of that meeting with XL in June 2006. "But I'd never heard of XL, so I thought I might be on my way to meeting an Internet perv."

Huggett and XL turned out to be legit. He admired her talent and presentation and listened intently while she talked about her musical leanings and attitudes. Huggett, in turn, brought Adele to the attention of XL founder Richard Russell, who, in a *Guardian* interview, agreed with Huggett's early assessment of Adele. "The idea of XL has always been to work with people who are original, and Adele has this ability to connect. There's something special about her voice and she is incredibly honest."

XL was being daring in their courtship of Adele, as were the other labels who had shown interest. And with good reason. Going into 2006, the music industry was in a quagmire. The downloading phenomena was slowly but surely eroding the power major labels had maintained for decades. A do-it-yourself mentality was on the march, with many bands finding alternatives to marketing their music without the necessity of label interest.

Serious musicians and songwriters were being largely shunted aside, especially in the pop arena, in favor of pre-teen cartoon figures with good looks but limited talent. This disposable state of affairs was made even more odious by the reliance on sex to sell even the reasonably talented female performers.

Bottom line: Adele was nothing like the prevailing industry standard. But Adele was exactly what XL was looking for.

The whirlwind courtship of Adele by XL continued when Huggett suggested that she meet with veteran manager Jonathan Dickins, who headed up the powerhouse firm September Management. As fate would have it, Dickins had only recently entered the world of Myspace and, on Huggett's recommendation, called up Adele's demo. Like Huggett, he was struck by the sincerity and emotional impact of her songs. He immediately agreed to meet with Adele.

Adele left Ben behind this time. This time she brought her mother along. All of a sudden, this was starting to feel a bit serious.

Dickins is old school in his approach to management. Not a lot of glitz, flash, and bombast. What he is, is very artist-friendly. It was that attitude that he brought to the table in his first meeting with the singer. Like all managers about to make his pitch, Dickins had done his homework. He knew she was eighteen, just out of the BRIT School, and wanted to be a singer. Repeated viewings of Adele's Myspace tape told him everything else he needed to know.

Adele and her mother were, admittedly, excited, as well as a bit apprehensive. It all seemed like a fairy tale that was about to have a happy ending, but Adele was reportedly apprehensive at the prospect of the other shoe dropping. However, Dickins was cordial, realistic, and most important, immediately attentive to the artistic needs of Adele.

"We discussed music in that first meeting," he told *Pollstar*. "I listened to what Adele wanted, and for a young girl, she seemed very focused on what she thought was right for her career. So I listened, threw in some ideas, and generally, it just clicked."

He remembered the meeting being one of the most simple, straightforward meetings he had ever conducted with a potential client, and not surprisingly, shortly after the meeting concluded, Dickins agreed to represent her.

Adele agreed as well, but her reasoning was typically Adele. He had made her laugh.

The inevitable deal with XL loomed large; Adele conceded in an interview with MOG that she was not sure that XL had totally gotten what she was about.

"When XL signed me, I think they thought I was going to be an acoustic artist," she said. "At the time, I had no choice but to be an acoustic artist because I didn't have the money to have a band. I really wanted to be a pop star. I think they thought I was going to be a lot more low-key than I would become."

On the other hand, XL knew exactly what they were getting in the bubbly, fresh-faced singer: straightforward, honest songs delivered in a powerful and, yes, original way. Admittedly, Adele was not as flamboyant or progressive an act as the label was used to signing. But she did meet an all-important XL requirement: Adele knew exactly what she was about musically and would require almost no hand-holding in the creative sense. Adele was ready to play.

It was a given that XL was the one and only suitor for Adele, and negotiations for her services went smoothly over the next three months. For Adele, the ensuing months were a whirlwind of exciting activity. She continued to play out, but with a new sense of excitement fueled by her impending success. Word spread through the musicians of the local scene, many of whom were already on the XL roster or managed by September Management. They were intensely supportive of Adele and assured her that she had made the right decision.

She was meeting new people and taking meetings with Dickins and other members of his staff. XL was attentive, supportive, and patient in guiding the young girl in the nuts and bolts of preparing a talented performer to meet the public. Adele took it all in. She asked all the right questions and proved to be a quick study in the ways of the music business. In her private moments, it all continued to feel unreal. Until the day . . .

"I never wanted to be famous," she related in an Interviews/Reviews Web site interview. "I only decided that I wanted to do this when I was offered the record deal over lunch. I was there with my manager and my mum and this guy from XL just kind of popped the question. We looked at each other and I said 'Yeah!'"

Adele signed on the dotted line with XL in September 2006. The day she signed her contract, she impulsively told XL President Richard Russell that all she wanted was a No. 1 record. Russell assured her that he would do everything possible to make that happen.

Adele's family and friends were thrilled, especially Adele's mother. Penny had always been the driving force in her daughter living her dreams, and Adele would always reinforce that fact. The record deal had only cemented their loving relationship. And Penny would be quite content to stay largely in the background of her daughter's career, showing her face on rare and special occasions while avoiding the dreaded "stage mother" label. Adele was in total agreement with her mother's approach to a celebrity daughter.

Adele told 411Mania that she was big on keeping her family and career at arm's length from each other. "My family is obviously a huge part of where I am now. My music and my career are very separate from my home life. I've never involved my family in it and they've never gotten in the way either."

By her own estimation, the advance Adele received from XL was humble, although she would joke at times about how it had been a million pounds. Whatever the amount, it was large enough for Adele to impulsively go on a shopping spree that ate up most of it. Her big splurge would be handbags.

Choosing to spend her advance money on handbags should not have come as much of a surprise. After all, Adele was only eighteen years old and, singing talent aside, was nothing more than a typical immature teenager who did not regret anything and felt that she knew it all. Adele may have been a star in the making, but she was still ego-driven and brash, a work in progress.

Adele took a small apartment near the XL offices for convenience's sake. But with the growing buzz, it was not long before the paparazzi got wind of Adele and, despite her relative obscurity, began stalking her like she was an A-list celebrity.

Adele was not used to this sudden attention, which led to some amusing moments. On one occasion she was greeted at the doorway of her flat by a photographer flashing away. Adele got mad and started swinging on the photographer. After the dust settled, the paparazzo sheepishly explained that he had mistaken her for Elle Macpherson who, coincidentally, happened to live in the neighborhood. Adele had to admit that was kind of funny. But it began to be a bit of a strain when she began spotting fans and photographers alike crawling around on the roof of her building. And finally, there was the day when an Adele encounter with another paparazzo ended up with punches being thrown.

"There was this one guy," she recalled in a *Washington Post* interview. "I had gone to the shop to buy bread, milk and cigarettes. I came back and he was on my doorstep, snapping a photo. I nearly beat the crap out of him. Since then, I haven't had the paparazzi at my house."

The irony of her paparazzi dustups was that Adele had long been a fan of the celebrity trash magazines and would often have a good laugh at her favorite celebrities being shown in a lesser light. But Adele had always been forthright about not wanting to be "out there and scandalous" and being shown in any way that would detract from her music. She told a *MiNDFOOD* interviewer that she had already cut off the tabloid sharks.

"The paparazzi aren't really that interested in me because I don't hide anything," she said. "I'm very honest and I don't keep secrets. I'd be the first person to admit I was scandalous. I'd put it on my blog."

Like every other element of the star-making machinery, she would eventually come to acknowledge that having flash cameras going off in her face was part of the process and would smile politely at the proper photo ops. However, she would make it plain with regularity that she valued her privacy and the ability to still walk the streets without being accosted, both elements of the non-celebrity world that she was realistic enough to know would soon disappear.

Many of those in Adele's inner circle had felt she had made an error in signing with XL rather than holding out for an offer by a major name-recognizable label . . . like, say, Virgin. But XL already had a reputation for being more aggressive in developing talent, and because they had a track record for being choosy in who they signed, they would make Adele a priority in the developing of her talent and getting her music in front of the people. What Adele would get from XL would most likely be slow in coming from a bigger label . . . and then only after she had achieved some initial success.

Lost in the excitement of her signing was the fact that, a month earlier, Adele had contributed two of her songs, "Daydreamer" and "My Same," to a small-circulation music and arts magazine called *Platforms*. In a short but effusive sidebar bio, the writer ended with the words "Certainly one to look out for."

But while someone to look out for, Adele continued to play her career low-key and true to her roots. With the weight of XL behind her, she could have barged to the front of the line and headlined in most clubs in London. But she continued to hone her performing skills in the shadows, often as the opening act.

She recalled one of those dues-paying gigs in a 2009 interview with *Vogue*. Jack Peñate had asked her to open for him at a small club called The Troubadour, a claustrophobic place on Earls Court, where a sellout show was 100 people.

"I went on first and I was on my own," she related. "It was packed, it was hot, it was disgusting. Then I began to sing and the room was silent. Then I saw these girls crying. I was like 'Oh my God!' This is amazing. I thought, 'There is nothing more freeing than playing live . . .'

"Nothing."

5

BOY ON HER CHEST

s if her eighteenth year was not already complicated enough, Adele chose that moment to fall in love for the very first time—with a boy who, to this day, Adele has refused to identify. One thing we do know . . .

Is that it was a first love gone terribly bad.

Adele had admitted on several occasions that, while wise to the way of the world on many levels, she was still a young girl when it came to affairs of the heart. Like most teen girls, Adele had her share of mild flirtations, relationships, and breakups throughout her high school years. She once quipped that one relationship ended when he cheated on her and she broke up with him with a text message.

But she had never come close to what would be considered a serious romance . . .

. . . until the mystery man entered her life. That's when she led with her heart.

Adele had known this boy for a while and, as these things often happen, friendship became something else on her eighteenth birthday. Adele had professed her love and the boy did the same. She knew he was bisexual but, in the rush of romance, felt they could somehow make it work. Four hours after laying their emotional cards on the table, the boy ran off to be with one of Adele's gay friends.

"Great!" Adele said in a moment of candor with an *Observer* reporter. "We were not even officially going out yet and you've cheated on me already!"

But Adele was willing to give this budding relationship, already off the rails, another chance. She had once indicated that she loved the drama surrounding boys who treated her badly and, during the four months of intense love and betrayal that followed, she would have more drama than she could handle.

He would continue to cheat. Adele would drink more than normal to salve the heartbreak. But ultimately it was the inability of having a relationship with a bisexual boy that pushed Adele to the edge.

"All the things I wanted from a boyfriend, he was never going to be," she declared in her official Web site biography. "I was jealous and I couldn't see myself fighting off boys and girls."

Adele went so far as to say that she sensed from the outset that the relationship was doomed when she rehashed it during a *Scotsman* interview. "He was a bit of a wrong 'un. But there's something spontaneous about wrong 'uns. You're surprised at the end that he was a wrong 'un."

By August 2006, the relationship was hanging by a thread.

And it came to a thudding conclusion in a pub at six A.M. one morning after the latest row resulting from the boyfriend's cheating. There were the expected heated words and angry accusations. Reportedly, Adele slapped her former lover across the face before taking off and running down a London street.

Adele was emotionally distraught with the breakup, but she had more pressing issues to deal with at the moment. Her record deal with XL was about to be finalized and the label would want her first album in a timely manner. There was only one problem: At the time of the breakup, she only had three songs. She needed more, and the only topic that would resonate with her at the moment was the heartache of the breakup, still very fresh in her thoughts and emotions. So she wrote about him.

And in the process, Adele found a silver lining in the pathos. "He made me an adult and put me on the road that I'm traveling," she told PopEater.

As listeners would later discover, Adele's first album, *19*, was very much a reflection of that relationship, and during a conversation with the *Daily Mail*, she gave every indication that her first serious relationship was very much in the past.

"I got an album out of him. I used him more than he used me."

6.

2007: AN ADELE ODYSSEY

Adele was now officially an artist on XL. But four months before the signing made front-page news, Adele was already causing a major stir.

Later . . . with Jools Holland had been a BBC institution long enough for Adele to have been a regular viewer as a young child. This showcase for established and on-the-rise music personalities had always been a tough nut to crack, and it was next to impossible to land an appearance without a record deal. But when Alison Howe, producer of *Later . . . with Jools Holland,* heard Adele's three-song demo, she jumped at the chance to make Adele that all-too-rare exception to the rule.

Adele was thrilled at the invite. When she found out that she would be sharing the program with Paul McCartney and Bjork, she recalled that she was suddenly "sick and terrified." Normally Adele would close her eyes when singing, but she was in such a state on this night that her eyes remained wide open during her emotional rendition of "Daydreamer."

"They usually put you in the middle of the room," she related in an interview with *The Guardian*. "But, for some reason, they put me on the end, right in front of the audience, with Bjork on my left and Paul McCartney on my right. My mum was in the audience and she was crying right in front of me. I met them (Bjork and McCartney) afterwards and I couldn't stop crying."

Adele's appearance on the show had the desired effect. Her growing legion of local London followers tuned in to see one of their own perform for the first time on network television. Those tuning in primarily to see McCartney and Bjork were most likely happily surprised at the performance by this unknown singer. XL was thrilled with the feedback and exposure, and smug in the idea that an unknown singer with no record to promote could land such a prestigious slot.

The next step was to begin getting the word out beyond the group of hipsters that had gotten her this far.

Which meant getting a record out. And it would be a very small step. When he was not putting out new music on the XL label and under the management umbrella of September Management, Jamie T ran a small boutique label called Pacemaker Records. Pacemaker was known for small runs of hip artists and had become the go-to source for hipsters looking for a first look at the next big thing.

On October 22, 2007, Pacemaker released Adele's first recorded effort, a two-sided seven-inch record featuring the songs "Hometown Glory" and "Best For Last." For a DIY indie effort, the record was more than a mere calling card for an emerging talent. Both songs showcased Adele as a largely formed talent with songwriting skills and a voice that was all the more powerful in this stripped-down musical setting.

The limited edition, five-hundred-record run became an instant collector's item and, while the single did not make the charts, it plugged into some good word of mouth.

"I couldn't believe how well that song did," she told Spyder's Random Things. "I'm so flattered that it was received so well because it was the first song that I ever wrote."

The Adele train had officially left the station.

The last two months of 2007 were a blur of activity. She was meeting with superstar producers, the likes of Mark Ronson, who had recently made magic with Amy Winehouse and the solid pop stylist Jim Abbiss. She was rounding into shape on new songs and keeping her performing chops up with sporadic shows in and around London. Word of mouth had quickly made Adele the one to see in a live setting, but she took great pains to just be part of the overall vibe of a show and not the uncrowned queen-of-pop-music in waiting.

She proved particularly adept at soothing a wild crowd at the Kings Road club Scala when, after rapper Lethal Bizzle had worked the audience into a frenzy, Adele calmly walked onto the stage carrying a guitar and a beer and broke up the audience when she indicated that she loved seeing an audience breathe. On a much grander scale, on the first night of the popular Electric Proms festival, she upstaged performances by members of The Charlatans and Kaiser Chiefs with a powerful performance that already had the press trumpeting her as the next Amy Winehouse.

Although flattered at the notion of being compared to someone of Winehouse's caliber, Adele was instinctively leery of such accolades and would continue to take great pains to emphasize her individual skills and be just as quick to dismiss critics who had already hinted that her favored status in signing with XL and the prime shot on *Later* . . . were part of a calculating venture to manufacture a pop star.

As busy as her life was becoming, Adele remained loyal to her circle of musicians and friends. When label-mate Jack Peñate suggested that she might want to contribute some backing vocals to his song "My Yvonne," she was in the studio like a shot. Working with a friend in a professional setting was the proverbial busman's holiday for the singer who fancied the notion of playing a supportive counter to her close friend's effort.

Adele turned in a sold-out charity performance at the annual MENCAP Little Noise Sessions on November 22, when she was part of an all-star lineup that included her personal favorites Will Young and Damien Rice. She talked to BBC Newsbeat prior to her performance about playing with people she admired, in particular the very first *Pop Idol* (the forerunner of *American Idol*) winner Will Young, and how nervous she was at the prospect of performing in such an intimate setting.

"I'm excited as well, but I'm really nervous. You can't really talk in the venue, so people are going to be concentrating on what I'm doing. My mum's coming, and four of my friends and their girlfriends. They usually heckle but, if they do it here, I will personally get offstage and punch them."

With the holidays approaching, Adele continued to be the

apple of the UK media's eye. December 7 saw the singer in top form as she mesmerized the *Friday Night with Jonathan Ross* television audience with a powerful rendition of "Chasing Pavements" and some spirited, good-natured patter.

Three days later, Adele would receive the first of many honors when the newly inaugurated category of the BRIT Critics Choice Awards honored Adele as the best emerging British talent that had not yet released a debut album. She acknowledged to Digital Spy, "I was a bit shocked. I didn't know anything about the award until I won it. But they're saying I'm good."

Adele had been surprised by the news because she had voluntarily gone into seclusion at the tail end of the year, rehearsing but basically enjoying the season and sticking close to home. "Over Christmas and New Year, I was with my mum and we weren't paying much attention to what was going on," she offered Spyder's Random Things. "I didn't notice the hype and I wasn't reading the press."

Adele would continue to revel in this first brush with popular acceptance, acting more the young inexperienced girl than anything resembling a seasoned performer.

"I'm really flattered to have won in this new category," she told *The Guardian*. "It's fantastic to have lots of people supporting me."

But winning the Critics Choice Award would not be a total lovefest. The first hint of a backlash came almost immediately with charges that the fledgling singer had been given this first-time-ever award because Adele had come from The BRIT School and that this was the first step down the road of becoming a manufactured pop star. Adele was uncomfortable with the criticism, as well as the idea of winning an award before even a first record was available and, not long after the ceremony, turned to singer and friend Robbie Williams for a pep talk.

"Robbie told me that the prize was a leg up," she told the *Daily Mail*, "and that it put me in a position where people would now listen to me. That helped."

The irony of closing out the year with this award was not lost on Adele. In less than thirty days she would not have qualified. Because in less than thirty days, the world would be hearing Adele's first album.

7.
HEY *19*

A dele went into a complete and utter funk in the wake of her breakup with her mystery beau. Her three early songs, "Hometown Glory," "Daydreamer," and "My Same," had gotten her in the door. But an EP was not what XL had in mind for her debut release, and she could not write another song to save her life. And it was a block that would last well into June of 2007.

By this time, Adele had been unofficially crowned the "next thing" in popular music and, in more extreme proclamations, the savior of the music industry. While she was grateful and encouraged by the tidal wave of positive press, she was also paranoid at the prospect of now having to deliver the goods.

"When they were tipping (hyping) me in 2007, I had hardly written any songs," she told the *Daily Mail*. "So I stepped back, got out of people's faces, and concentrated on making a good record."

The easy outs of being on the road and hotel life, hanging out in clubs, and meeting Mr. Right on a moonlit night were clichés that Adele could not stomach as she struggled with her own demons while writing for her first album. "I'm actually offended by literal, easy lyrics that have no thought behind them," she told *Blues & Soul*.

But as she struggled with inspiration, there most certainly must have been those moments when an easy-out love song or a hip cover song would have sounded awfully tempting. But that's the kind of thing most critics expected of a first-time recording artist. Adele was determined to not be what people expected.

The singer was determined to do things her way, but Adele was feeling the pressure. XL had a sterling reputation for giving their artists all the time they needed and were certainly not going to rush her. However, the label had already invested a lot of time and money in her, and while they were supportive and encouraging, the clock was definitely ticking on her debut album.

That's when Adele looked in the mirror and found inspiration in her immediate past.

"I had gotten into a relationship that had gone very sour," she remarked to *Blues & Soul*. "But yeah, as cheesy as it sounds, I wrote about him and how awful everything had been, and kind of cleansed myself of all that and got it out of my system."

And getting her emotions out of her system turned out to

be a real ordeal. She had admitted on several occasions to locking herself in her house, drinking massive amounts of alcohol, and then jotting down her innermost thoughts in what she called her "drunk diary." It would be a safe bet that several of the songs that would appear on her debut album would be formed in the same sort of way.

In a matter of months, Adele had written a dozen odes to melancholy and lost love. Songs that, she reasoned, would truly complement her big, soulful vocals. The hurt was still there and there were, doubtless, tears that fell as she was writing them. But, she reasoned, it would disappear by the time *19* was released. Adele knew that she was going against the public's perceived notions of young, inexperienced singer-songwriters that were formed by those being turned out by other writers and producers. But Adele had always pointed with pride to the fact that nearly all the songs on her debut album were written by her, and she has bristled at the notion that she is anything but a creditable artist.

However, she has admitted that gearing up for the recording of her debut album, she was a bit lost. Being a pop star had always been fun and games. Now the fantasy was out the window, pop stardom was hard work, and that was the side of things she was still coming to grips with. She had danced around the notion of what the album title, *19,* meant before acknowledging that between the ages of eighteen and nineteen she had grown into a woman. But she was basically clueless about what would become of her maiden voyage beyond just making a record and getting an old boyfriend off her chest.

She explained to Blogcritics that the way she was writing for *19* was pretty much how she had always written. Sometimes it was a reality check in which she would force herself to write, which usually resulted in little or no success.

"If I try and make myself write, nothing ever comes," she said. "It's usually at four a.m., when I get up to use the toilet or get a glass of water, that an idea comes and I have to sit down to pursue it."

During this period, Adele took some time off to collaborate on what would be a duet with old friend Jamie T. It was a welcome side project that was never completed.

XL was thrilled when they were presented with Adele's batch of songs. They fit in with their perception of the young singer as a traditional soul singer with definite pop sensibilities. Certain songs appeared to quite naturally equate with the prevailing pop and electro elements of new music while others were enticingly simple and evocative of times gone by. The record company saw hits and sales and a monster success.

Despite their notions of what the perfect Adele album should be, management and label people knew better than to shove any suggestions down Adele's throat. And so, ultimately, it was left up to their nineteen-year-old singer to make an album she felt comfortable with.

Which, as the weeks of recording went by, translated into sparse studio settings and a limited array of instruments. It would be rare during the sessions that there would be another musician in the room. Suggestions were tossed back and forth matter-of-factly. Adele's success in the studio would ultimately hinge on her comfort level.

The singer would later concede in an eMusic interview that she went into the recording of *19* with a very limited musical vocabulary. "I wrote about ninety percent of the first record on my own. It was all very stripped back and acoustic. In terms of musicianship I was very limited."

Which is why her manager, Jonathan Dickins, may well have been taking a chance when he suggested to Adele that an old Bob Dylan chestnut, "Make You Feel My Love," might fit well in her creative world. Dickins had been persistent, going on about the song for the better part of a year, before Adele would consider doing a cover, even one with the pedigree of being a Dylan composition.

But doing a cover of a Bob Dylan song was not an easy sell, as Adele explained in an interview with MyPlay. "When I first heard it, I couldn't understand the lyrics. But, when I finally read them, I thought they were amazing. The song just kind of summed up that sour period in my life."

"Make You Feel My Love" would end up making the album. Adele would often explain that even with the specter of her first album staring her in the face, she still remained very much a fan of all music rather than an artist caught up completely in her world.

As she prepared to begin recording, Adele was intent on making the best album she could. How successful it would be was a whole other matter.

"I thought it would be a London thing," Adele predicted to *BlackBook* magazine. "I certainly did not think it would travel anywhere else."

Looking to copper their bet on an album that would have massive appeal, XL brought in a cadre of seasoned hip producers. Jim Abbiss had made his bones producing the likes of The Arctic Monkeys, The Sneaker Pimps, and Kasabian. Eg White, a long-standing producer/songwriter/musician, had been involved with a literal who's who of the UK British pop movement and had worked his magic with the likes of James Blunt, Will Young, and Duffy.

And then there was Mark Ronson, who was brought in to work a particular brand of magic for Adele.

The XL people felt that the album needed something fast and, yes, somewhat commercial, to balance out the slower tempo, introspective songs, and they felt "Cold Shoulder" was a prime candidate. But, as presented by Adele, "Cold Shoulder" was a fairly bare-bones song with no beats to speak of. It was suggested that Mark Ronson would be ideal to come in and produce a more upbeat "Cold Shoulder." Adele knew enough about Ronson to instantly agree.

Ronson had been the hot young turk in British pop circles for quite some time. Of late, the rest of the world had come to know him on the strength of the late Amy Winehouse's album *Back To Black*. But Adele was deeper into the scene and would rave about Ronson's earlier works like *Version* and *Here Comes the Fuzz*. It seemed like a match made in heaven.

Like all in-demand producers, Ronson did his homework. He listened to her demo, talked to people who knew her and had seen her perform, and researched the pedigree of performers who were signed to XL. There remained one more hurdle to jump before a deal was sealed.

The producer had a policy of meeting with a person before he decided to work with them, and so, on the day in question, Adele and he scheduled an informal get-together. Unfortunately, Ronson had forgotten about the meeting, and once he did show up, he was greeted with a disconcerting sight. Adele had been drinking and smoking and, when he walked in, he found her drunk and bleary-eyed with her face on the television screen, watching *The Jerry Springer Show*. Ronson was not thrilled.

Adele recalled that "there were some awkward moments" but eventually they got down to business and eased into a level of creative honesty that sealed the deal.

"She said, 'This is the song I want you to produce,'" he told the *London Evening Standard*. "I was struck by her determination as well as her talent. It's great when a person comes along with a great voice and great songs. It trumps everything."

The trade-off between Adele and Ronson was simple: her voice and the power of the lyrics took center stage, with the producer delicately layering on the beats. By the time Adele and Ronson had convened in the recording studio, all the creative preliminaries had been taken care of and all-important trust had been established. Consequently, when Ronson suggested that former Jamiroquai bassist Stuart Zender be brought into the studio to beef things up, the singer readily agreed. The results were emotional and hypnotic. Ronson was in and out of the session fairly quickly with a job well done.

Things would take a more dramatic and immediate turn when Eg White entered the recording process. White was known for his ability to give the artist's material free rein while adding orchestral and textural flourishes to the production, a trait he would perform admirably on the *19* songs "Tired" and "Melt My Heart To Stone." What he could not have predicted was that he would become a participant in

Adele's own personal angst when it came to the breakout song "Chasing Pavements."

Adele had long been debating with herself about the importance of having at least one blatantly commercial, radio-friendly song on *19,* which was why she had sought out White in the first place. That was intentional. How the scenario would ultimately play out was not.

The day before, Adele had had the infamous final blowup with her boyfriend and, in her frustration, had hastily written down a couple of what she termed "shitty chords." It was not her finest emotional moment, but she knew enough about Eg White's ability to show up at his studio bright and early the next morning. White told *The Telegraph* blog what happened next.

"Adele came in and she said, 'I wanna write a big hit, slushy ballad like a Goo Goo Dolls song.' I said, 'You've come to the right man, let's nail it.'"

Adele sat down in a corner of White's cluttered studio and, with the producer's subtle poking and prodding, emerged from her emotional funk with the song "Chasing Pavements."

White's approach of "working with singers" rather than "for singers" resulted in three killer songs based around Adele's natural abilities and White's talents at orchestrating the proper mood. And at the end of the day, the very lush, Burt Bacharach–styled production values would succeed in giving Adele her hit.

By comparison, it would seem that Abbiss may have had the easier time of it. If the final result was any indication, it was a smooth transition from style to style; balancing out the appropriate arrangements on fully half a dozen songs and bringing true luster to what would be the breakout songs "Daydreamer" and "Hometown Glory," and the powerful emotional turns on "Make You Feel My Love" and "Right As Rain."

Abbiss told *HUB* magazine that it was actually as smooth a process as could be. "She would be having a cup of something, chatting about *EastEnders* (a popular UK TV show). But as soon as the recording light went on, some amazing music would pour out of her."

Ultimately, what may have been the truest challenge for Adele in the making of *19* was the song "Right As Rain," which she cowrote with the songwriting production team Truth And Soul, which consisted of no less than four other writers (Leon Marcus Michels, Jeff Silverman, Clay Holley, and Nick Movshon). Given her solitary nature and insistence on writing her own songs, one can only imagine how she went about the collaboration process. It all seemed to have worked out, as "Right As Rain" would prove to be both entertaining and endearing in a soul/pop way. And an indication that, creatively, Adele could get along well with others while maintaining her individuality.

19 was completed in October 2007. While the producers commenced with postproduction, Adele was free to unwind. She did a handful of live shows in which she gave a couple of powerful teasers of what would be in the grooves of *19*. She had also become fast friends with Mark Ronson and had spent a couple of nights barhopping in some of the trendier spots in New York.

But her thoughts were never far from the completed album. She was in constant contact with XL Recordings and

September Management for the latest bits of news. The buzz was already beginning to build behind the album. The press, and most important, the press outside the UK, was beginning to perk up their ears. And that was perfectly fine with Adele, whose outgoing nature and willingness to do any and all press was a marketing plus.

Adele was particularly happy with the results of the album. She knew that in pop music circles, it was the rare emerging artist who had the opportunity to write a first album primarily of their own songs. She looked at the fact that the songs were all hers as a sign of respect.

The consensus of those in and around the recording of *19* was that Adele was effectively walking a fine line between on-the-job training and being a nineteen-year-old girl ego-tripping with the possibilities that had been handed her. In a conversation with Spinner, Adele acknowledged the latter.

"I was very much a teenager and I thought I knew it all. But that's what happens when you're nineteen and you're making your first record."

But as often happens with an album so based in simplicity, reviewers would continue to dissect *19* looking for that all-important something. Adele laughed off the notion of there being "something more" to *19* in a conversation with Blogcritics.

"It's a breakup record," she chuckled. "It's a breakup record from the very bottom of my soul. As cheesy as that sounds."

But Adele would admit in a conversation with *Venus Zine* that *19* brought her to a doorway that was ultimately not easy to pass through. "On *19* I had to admit things to myself that I really didn't want to hear. I could glamorize all the shitty stuff all I wanted but there was also so many times that I was shocked by how pathetic I felt."

Adele braced herself for the inevitable frenzy that would be the run-up to the release of *19*. She had already received the first trickle of descriptions and comparisons. She had gotten signed because labels were looking for the next Amy Winehouse. That she, and the likes of fellow singer Duffy, were part of a seemingly gimmicky return to white-girl soul. In her own head, Adele was already well rehearsed in her responses.

"I'm a big fan (of Winehouse) and I'm flattered by the comparison," she told *Time Out London*. "But I'm not copying Amy and I did not make a Motown album."

Adele was more overwhelmed and, perhaps, not quite prepared for the flood of unadulterated hype hitting the US blogs. Famed US gossip columnist Perez Hilton had pretty much ordained her the second coming, and superstar Kanye West's Twitter line was burning overtime with praise. Without the benefit of actual songs for people to hear, Adele was both grateful and concerned when she talked to *Time Out London*.

"The industry over there knew about me but none of the public did," she said. "There's a lot being said. I was not planning on going over to the States until May."

But now it looked like Adele would have to come a lot sooner.

8

GOOD TIMES ... BAD TIMES

t was a good omen.

On January 14, 2008, Adele's second official single and the first tied specifically to the debut of the album *19* was released. It would rise to No. 1 on the UK singles charts and remain there for four weeks.

19 followed on January 28. It would be an immediate critical success. Reviewers lined up to cast their raves for the Etta James–inspired "My Same," the soulful melody of "Make You Feel My Love," and the urgent underpinnings of "Tired." Every song on the album found its champion and no review ever ventured far from the notion that *19* was a very real exercise in very real emotions.

The Guardian stated that "The way she stretched her vocals, her wonderful soulful phrasing, and the sheer unadulterated pleasure of her voice stood out all the more."

BBC Music offered, "She's included something for everyone without pandering to a single trend."

People magazine said, "With a knockout voice that's rich and supple, robust and sultry, it's hard to believe that this singer-songwriter is barely out of her teens."

Billboard opined, "Adele truly has the potential to become among the most respected and inspiring international artists of her generation."

However, not everybody was enamored of *19*. Some of the crustier, old-line critics felt that the album was overly melodramatic and oppressive. Some dismissed *19* as an overly trendy and insubstantial exercise. And then there were those reviews that praised Adele with a backhand when they ordained her the next Amy Winehouse. But the bottom line was that, from the onset, *19* was a major success all over the world, spawning sales, airplay, and a growing legion of fans clamoring for more Adele.

By the time the dust settled on the early and immediate success of *19* in the UK and much of the rest of the world, Adele was experiencing the joy of a chart-busting debut and the reality of pushing an album into the public consciousness.

January saw Adele on a near daily diet of press during the day and performances at night. The singer was drawn to the excitement of it all, and she was not above letting her audience know what she was going through.

"I'm sorry if I pass out," she laughingly said in a review/report filed by *The Guardian*. "I've had no sleep. My record company thought it would be a good idea for me to be on *Good Morning* TV and my hands are shaking from too much black coffee."

But overwork would not be an excuse on February 6, 2009, in Los Angeles, when Adele, on a quick flight across the pond, was part of an all-star tribute to Neil Diamond as part of the MusiCares: Person of the Year awards program. Adele was both honored and anxious to be performing on stage with the likes of Coldplay, The Red Hot Chili Peppers, and Lucinda Williams. She had been selected to sing Diamond's classic "Cracklin' Rosie."

However, things turned bloody ugly when, just prior to her performance, she ripped a nail on her thumb.

"I had to wrap a tampon on my thumb to soak up the blood," she lamented to *The Sunday Times*. "And because all my dresses were in the dry cleaners, I had to go on stage in my coat. I was going to grip the microphone in my other hand but I got so stressed that I held the microphone with the hand with the tampon on it. There it was, right up in front of my face."

Adele offered that, as if things could not get any worse, "I had trouble remembering the words and my voice was not right for the song. I was so mortified. My performance was fucking rubbish."

Looming over Adele was the inevitable test of how big she could possibly be: her first tour of the United States. There had always been a cache about the British coming to America. They did not call the arrival of The Beatles and other acts in the '60s "The British Invasion" for nothing. If you could make it in America, long-standing popularity was assured—which was why there was more than a little concern when early reports of sales of *19* were very good . . .

Everywhere except the United States.

Despite an aggressive marketing campaign by XL, the album had gotten off to a sluggish start in America, debuting at No. 56 on the Billboard charts. As the weeks went by, *19* continued to be mired in the lower depths of Billboard album sales.

The slow start in the States was due, in part, to the immediate controversy that sprang up around the single "Chasing Pavements." A misguided blogger posted a note saying that the term "chasing pavements" was slang for chasing after gay men. Several US radio stations refused to play the song for that reason, and by the time Adele and her people countered with the spirited defense of what the title really meant, it was too late. "Chasing Pavements" would ultimately rise to only a respectable No. 21 on the Billboard charts.

Adele's team did not want to antagonize the US fans right out of the box. But the reality was that American audiences had become so saturated with the Lady Gagas and spectacle performers that they seemed to prefer style over actual musical substance. Expressed in hushed tones was the notion that a performer who relied on pure talent rather than revealing costumes and stage pyro effects was going to have a hard struggle.

Management was quick to take notice of her stumbling start in America. The rest of the world getting Adele was the icing on the cake, but in order for Adele to claim the prize of stardom, America would have to fall in line. Jonathan Dickins knew the importance of capturing the US market, but knowing the emotional makeup of Adele, he did not want to burden her with that concern so early in the game. Conversations concerning America were limited to those between himself and XL Recordings.

In the meantime, Adele mania was in full swing, and the

singer conceded in a TwitLonger Web site piece, "My rise to popularity was so fast I couldn't keep up with it. I hadn't had any time to adjust to how I felt about it. It was such a whirlwind, I forgot about why I was doing it."

It was easy to see why Adele was having such a hard time bringing it all into focus. She had kicked off 2008 with a seemingly endless round of promotional tours to different countries, endless rounds of press interviews, and all the trappings of the star-making machinery. And it was to her credit that she never faltered in these duties. Her enthusiasm was infectious. Going on twenty, she was in many ways still a young, rough-around-the-edges, cockney girl. And the world was eating it up.

In preparation for the release of *19*, Adele opted for a short four-show tour, between January 27 and February 2, of London, Manchester, Birmingham, and Glasgow to keep her performing chops up for what was assumed would be a lengthier tour sometime in the new year.

While word of Adele's talents would be slow in reaching music lovers, the business line between XL and major US labels was burning up. Interest was high for the opportunity to have this lone female singer-songwriter on their roster. Consequently, a bidding war erupted between several labels to acquire the distribution rights to a total unknown with only one album to her name.

A March distribution deal between XL and Columbia in the United States was considered a good move for both sides. Columbia had long been a rock in the history of recorded music, attracting and holding some of the biggest names in the business. But while they went through a stage where they were being considered a bit stodgy in the face of new music and new attitudes, they had rebounded nicely in the '90s with the addition of fresher creative faces such as Rick Rubin and Steve Barnett. For Adele, the ability of a label like Columbia to get her music out and across the States was invaluable.

But even as the deal with Columbia was struck, there were questions. American labels had gotten very safe and conservative in their signings in recent years, and the result had been a flurry of insubstantial preteen pop, family-friendly hip-hop, and country that seemed more pop than country. Bottom line, most new music in the States was largely forgettable. And while the notion of a single female songwriter belting out soulful blues had not completely disappeared off the radar, it had been relegated to a back burner. Both sides were taking a risk that Columbia could deliver the goods.

Adele did a quick hop to the States for a handful of intimate showcases in New York, Toronto, and Los Angeles to grease the wheels for the Columbia deal as well as to prime the pump for any future tour of the States.

Adele experienced the sights and sounds of a US tour for the first time. She embraced it with open arms and, in an interview with *The Sun,* had a good laugh at the expense of US perceptions of the British.

"American people think I am posh even though I am really not. They think I have a very British accent, as in 'Do you know the Queen?' I just laugh at them because, in England, I am thought of as common as muck."

Performances after the American shows literally ground to a halt. There were reports that Adele was spotted in and around London, either at a club in support of a fellow performer or just walking the streets on a day of shopping.

During this period, Adele once again went into the studio in support of musicians she admired when she handled vocal duties on a Raconteurs' cut called "Many Shades of Black," which would appear on the album *Consolers of the Lonely*. Adele recalled in an interview with BBC Newsbeat that she was excited at the possibility of working with band member Jack White (White Stripes).

"I thought I would never meet him. I was originally going to record with him in Nashville, but then he had to go do the Bond tune with Alicia Keyes. But then the band came to London to record at the Shepherd's Bush studio and we did it (the song) and it was lovely."

But as far as performing and making that leap from small-time club singer to headlining star, the team had bigger things in store.

One of those would be an immediate test of Adele's already much-publicized stage fright, an appearance at the April 2008 Coachella Valley Music and Arts Festival. Coachella was the modern version of Woodstock in a more controlled environment. Over the three days of the 2008 festival, the likes of Roger Waters, Kate Nash, and more than a couple of hundred musical performers would strut their stuff on various stages scattered around the festival grounds.

Adele's resolve was immediately tested when she entered the festival grounds and saw people as far as the eye could see. But she summoned up her courage and, by all accounts, put on a solid performance. Coachella did not immediately cure her stage fright, but it was a good first step and an introduction to the large appreciative audiences that performers at the height of their prowess could expect . . .

On a world tour.

On the surface, it seemed like a risky venture to invest the time, money, and logistics in mounting a headlining tour for a raw rookie with one album under her belt. Logic would seem to dictate a smallish club tour or as an opening act with a complementary headliner. That was certainly the way the major labels would handle it. But Adele's handlers had looked at the bottom line and, with the exception of the nagging inconsistency of the States, *19* was well on the way to platinum status within weeks of its release.

So more than one observer of the scene lifted an eyebrow when An Evening with Adele was conceived with risk written all over it. Scheduled to begin on May 23, 2008, and conclude on June 29, 2009, the projected fifty-one–date tour would, with the exception of two festival appearances, bypass her strong UK base of support in favor of a tour that would be bookended by forty North American dates, a frontal assault on the United States at the expense of more shows in what were considered already-conquered territories in the rest of the world. The tour would also take in two dates in Asia and nine in Europe. With the exception of the festival appearances, An Evening With Adele would concentrate on more intimate venues, primarily medium-sized clubs and concert halls of under 5,000 seats. As the tour would progress and ticket sales dictated, some of the tour stops would ultimately be scaled up but *small* remained the operative word.

As expected, the fifteen-song set list would concentrate

on songs from *19* and the odd cover thrown in that would often consist of chestnuts by her main inspiration, Etta James.

Dickins was an old hand at tour preparation at this point. He was well aware of the fact that Adele was quite young, vulnerable, and would be experiencing a number of firsts on her maiden voyage as a big-time performer. Which was why his first orders of business were to secure a topflight tour manager and, equally important, a solid personal assistant for his singer. Comfort would be the watchword. Dickins would also make a point of coming to America with regularity to get a firsthand look at how the tour was going and to make any suggestions or adjustments as needed.

Adele's debut album had quickly become a hip critics' favorite and resulted in some early-in-the-year awards as she captured honors in the BRIT Critics Choice Awards and the BBC's Sound of 2008, furthering cementing her reputation as the UK's shining light.

The obvious strengths of *19*, coupled with this latest wave of awards, were an important element in establishing her as a long-term legitimate performer of merit and inching her away from the still-lingering perception of being a manufactured performer.

The days and weeks counted down to the beginning of the tour. There were rehearsals and new band members to break in. Adele's ease with the process was such that anybody wandering into those rehearsals would most likely have seen Adele moving speakers or adjusting microphones. There was no diva in this girl.

By this time, Adele had become adept at dealing with the

rush of pre-tour interviews, charming the press with her candor and her sincerity.

And it was her honesty that led to the first reports that Adele was once again in a serious relationship. Word on this mystery beau was sketchy. He was a much older man, very worldly, and had opened her eyes to much different experiences. The relationship stories helped generate interest in the singer's serious musical aspirations, as did such minutiae as the particulars of Adele's tour rider, particulars that would include cigarettes, alcohol, specially made sandwiches, and bite-sized chocolate bars.

Adele celebrated her twentieth birthday in grand style with two sold-out shows at London's famed Shepherd's Bush Empire Theatre. At twenty she had come of age as a woman and was on the verge, exactly two years removed from BRIT, of a whole new adventure, one that had seen the singer go from an opening act to a much-publicized headliner. For Adele, it was a lot to take in.

She would later explain in an *Out* magazine interview that she had been concerned that those early shows would not sell out "but then the Shepherd's Bush shows sold out in ten seconds."

A third single, "Cold Shoulder," was released in April, primarily in Europe. A fourth and final single from *19*, "Make You Feel My Love," would follow in September. Both songs landed high on music charts in many countries and added fuel to Adele's prowess as a performer with a worldwide fan base.

The Evening with Adele tour began on May 21, 2008, in Los Angeles at the famed Roxy Theatre. The Roxy is a small

Adele strums on stage as part
of the Great Escape Festival in
Brighton, England. May 19, 2007.
(Dave Ethridge-Barnes/Getty)

osing for a photo shoot in the
Netherlands. March 5, 2008.
(Paul Bergen/Getty Images)

On stage during the 42nd Montreux Jazz Festival in Montreux, Switzerland. July 12, 2008 (Sandro Campardo/AP Photo/Keystone)

Flashing a smile at the Keep a Child Alive annual Black Ball benefit event New York City. November 13, 2008. (Andy Kropa/AP Photo)

...forming in the Sound studios in London. December 5, 2008. (Mark Allen/Getty Images)

Accepting the 2009 Grammy Award for Best New Artist. February 8, 2009. (Mark J. Terrill/AP Photo)

Chatting with Carson Daly on his NBC show *Last Call with Carson Daly*. February 10, 2009. (Stacie McChesney/NBC/NBCU Photo Bank via Getty Images)

Outside the Heineken Music Hall in Amsterdam, Netherlands. April 19, 2009. (Paul Bergen/Getty Images)

Signing autographs during her visit to *The Late Show with David Letterman* in New York City. February 21, 2011. (Dave Kotinsky/Getty Images)

stage at the MTV Video Music Awards in Los Angeles. August 28, 2011. (Matt Sayles/AP Photo)

On tour in Hamburg, Germany, shortly before announcing a break to repair a vocal cord hemorrhage. March 26, 2011. (Malte Christian/EPA/Newscom)

Adele's comeback performance at the 54th Annual Grammy Awards in Los Angeles. February 12, 2012. (Matt Sayles/AP Photo)

Sweeping the 2012 Grammys with six awards, including Song, Record, and Album of the Year. February 12, 2012. (Mark J. Terrill/AP Photo)

Paul McCartney congratulates
Adele backstage at the Grammys.
(Kevin Mazur/WireImage)

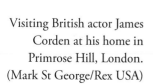

Visiting British actor James
Corden at his home in
Primrose Hill, London.
(Mark St George/Rex USA)

On stage during the Brit Awards 2012 in London. February 21, 2012. (Jonathan Short AP Photo)

Winning the award for Best British Female Solo Artist. February 21, 2012. (Joel Ryan AP Photo)

but important venue on the famed Sunset Strip and was legendary for sponsoring a three-night run by the then little-known Bruce Springsteen that would rocket him to stardom. Adele's handlers were hoping that lightning would strike twice.

From all reports, The Roxy was a good way to start the tour. Adele came across as delightfully human to an audience that had seen it all, and nobody could argue that the passion in her performance was anything but real. Reviews were effusive in their praise.

Then it was a quick jump to Vancouver, Canada, and the beginning of a hectic May-June jaunt from the US Pacific coast to the east.

American audiences responded in a big way to Adele. The singer's real-world approach to performing, the heartfelt simple songs, the between-song patter and, yes, the almost nightly battle with nerves were miles removed from the often plastic and condescending nature of the current state of pop music performers. This attitude was particularly appreciated in the smaller venues in the not-so-large cities where the main attraction, historically, had always been the music and not the spectacle. No shows stood out over the others. For Adele, every night was a highlight.

Adele easily flew in the face of being hip, cool, and condescending with nightly tales of drinking too much, the occasional flubbing of lyrics, and how homesick she was and how she missed her mom. She would have them rolling in the aisles when she admonished the audience to sit down because it was hard to dance to her songs.

And of course there were those songs, the emotional

journeys that cut through contrivance and found a home with audiences who could easily relate.

Adele's first foray into big-time performing could not have been going better. But the tour would sometimes have its bumps.

Adele had become so wrapped up in the emotion and inspiration of her music that it was not uncommon during the *19* tour for Adele to barely get through certain songs without a tear or a crack in her voice. Adele would often feel embarrassed at those onstage lapses. But the reality was that audiences were so drawn into the pathos and longing that the singer projected that they were enthralled at her honesty and, yes, humanity.

Of course, there was the reality of a tour to contend with. Adele was certainly not at the level where she could go first class all the way. The trappings of An Evening with Adele were spartan, to say the least. Long bus rides with what Adele laughingly told *The Telegraph* "were six stinky guys." The motels on tour stops were often roach-infested. These realities were easily balanced out by the camaraderie born of long hours, good drink, and good cheer.

Boredom was often the watchword. They quickly ran out of DVDs to watch. YouTube became the go-to visual entertainment. When she was upbeat, Adele was listening to a lot of Bruce Springsteen. When she was feeling sad, she popped Whitney Houston in. And there was a lot of Whitney in Adele's life during those endless bus rides.

"Yeah I was homesick," she candidly said to *Brightest Young Things*. "I missed my mum, my mates, my house, just getting to do whatever I wanted and to go where I wanted to go."

However, she also pointed out in a *Telegraph* interview that being thousands of miles from family and friends also had its upside. "When I get in a work mode I tend to just take charge on the road. That was a side of me that I didn't really want my family and friends to see."

From a creative point of view, the tour had its emotional bumps for the singer as well. Always thinking ahead, Adele had been convinced that she could write while on tour and was already thinking in terms of material for the follow-up to *19*. But what she discovered was the tour only contributed to a bad case of writer's block.

When she was not preoccupied with the business of touring, Adele was sleeping. Even when she had the time to be off by herself, the notion of writing a song was usually the farthest thing from her mind. And when it wasn't, the results were less than ideal. By her own estimation, Adele wrote six songs during the *19* tour, four of which she considered bad and just two alright.

"I always hoped that I could write on the road," she recalled in a *Q* interview, "but I couldn't do it."

Adele was also getting a hint of how celebrity flies in the big and small cities. Autograph seekers were everywhere and she readily signed. Then there were the paparazzi, the true chronicle of a person's climb to celebrity in a world saturated by pop culture. They seemed to be everywhere. Adele was a bit leery of this kind of intrusion and would often find herself being chased down the street or hiding in a bar, from where she would emerge, sometime later, feeling no pain.

Adele had come to love the States during the early stages of the tour. So much so that, during her rare time off, she would poke around big-city streets and consider the possibilities of getting a place somewhere in America to hole up and write her next album.

While the tour of the States was a wildly critical success, all the positive reviews in the world could not prevent *19* from continuing to be mired in the depths of the Billboard charts. It would take something truly magic to pull that rabbit out of a hat and, to that point, nobody in Adele's team had found the answer.

September 2008: the Evening With Adele tour goes off the rails.

Adele liked to party, and Adele with a drink in her hand was part of the nonperformance lifestyle during the 2008 tour. Whether she was drinking to excess was a question only discussed in whispers by members of the tour. Jonathan Dickins came to the States at several points to monitor the tour logistics and to check on Adele, and he never hinted at any problems. It would all seem moot because the singer was more than capable of putting on a first-rate show no matter how hard she partied the night before.

So it came as a surprise when Adele announced that she was canceling the all-important September US tour dates to return to London to deal with some "family matters." The excuse was paper thin and more than a bit suspect. The more cynical media was quick to pile on, offering that for the very young Adele it was simply a case of too much too soon, and that she was simply too immature to deal with the rigors of stardom.

Adele remained mum on the subject, and when she returned to the tour in a matter of weeks, the incident went largely by the wayside. But the seed of doubt about Adele's emotional durability had been planted and all the great performances would not make it go away.

Midway through October, the Evening with Adele tour had made its way to New York, where a golden opportunity awaited Adele. She was invited to appear on *Saturday Night Live*. The producers of the wildly popular and terminally hip television show had spent decades presenting to the world the latest in up-and-coming musical talent of the day. A modern-day offshoot of the old *Ed Sullivan Show* in a musical sense, *SNL* was known in music circles as the show that could make a career. Or, in the case of Adele, turn slow US interest into massive and instant popularity.

Adele and her management readily accepted the invite. Adele was well aware of the mixture of comedy and music that had made *SNL* a pioneer in late-night television. That it was terminally hip to Adele's way of thinking and regularly featured some of her favorite celebrity personalities was a bonus. She thought it would be a hoot.

Jonathan Dickins saw the appearance as something else. He admitted in a TwitLonger piece that he was reluctant to let Adele know what was really at stake with her *Saturday Night Live* appearance.

"You can put someone on a very big show but they still have to connect," he said. "It's not a given that going on a big show means you're going to break. You have to go on that show and connect with people."

Adele was in the moment as she sat in her dressing room, getting her makeup done as she waited for her call to the *Saturday Night Live* stage. She was starstruck by the fact that people like Alec Baldwin, Marky Mark, Tina Fey, and even former Republican vice-presidential candidate Sarah Palin were in the house. Adele recalled that she could feel the buzz and the electricity and sensed that this could be a career-making moment for her.

Adele would lead with her strengths that night, singing "Chasing Pavements" and "Cold Shoulder" to an enthusiastic studio audience. There was the expected glad-handing and congratulations after the show, but Adele, ever the perfectionist, did not feel she had given her best performance.

But good or bad, the reality was that an estimated 14 million people had tuned in to see Adele that night. By the next day, the true impact of Adele's appearance was apparent.

19 had jumped from No. 40 on the all-important iTunes charts to No. 1. Her current single, "Chasing Pavements," had jumped into the Top 25 of the coveted Billboard singles charts, while 19 jumped from its middling No. 46 position to No. 11, reportedly on the strength of ten thousand copies of the album selling literally overnight.

Adele was officially a star in America.

But as the tour continued through the end of the year, it was reported that Adele was having problems with alcohol. It was a given that she was a good-time girl who always seemed to have a drink in her hand. And while she was still wowing them on tour, there was growing concern that her continued drinking might be turning into full-blown alcoholism. Adele would occasionally address the issue, saying that she drank out of boredom and the fact that everywhere she went there was free beer but that she was not overdoing it.

Then it was up to people to believe what they wanted to believe.

But while alcohol may have been the cause, her constant state of stress, brought on to a large extent by her acknowledged ongoing stage fright as well as her acknowledgment that she was basically homesick and missing her mother, was the effect. But a rising star falling victim to booze was a much easier story for the tabloid press to sell to its readers than a star throwing up some nights before a performance. The reality was that, in a very large sense, Adele was still a young girl whose lifelong insecurities were being fueled by her current status as celebrity.

Consequently, when Adele unexpectedly moved out of her mother's house in November 2008 and into her own apartment in Notting Hill, the press painted a sinister portrait of a personal life in shambles and reported that the move was an attempt to give up drinking, when the reality was that Adele was just looking for independence.

It was a noble experiment that quickly failed.

"I found that I could not function without my mum," she was quoted as saying in Showbiz Spy, acknowledging that stress was a big part of her life. "I moved to Notting Hill to be on my own, but my life fell apart. My phone got cut off, my credit card got cut off, my house was a mess. It was awful. I couldn't function without my mum and so I moved back in with her."

Adele's failed attempt at independence quickly disappeared from the press as the Evening With Adele tour continued to rack up rave notices and record sales. Manager Dickins had been known to remark during this period and in a *Hitmakers* interview that "The reviews had been so incredible that it was like I had written them myself."

When the Evening with Adele tour resumed early in 2009, soundman Joe Zavaglia was now on board. From a technological point of view, Zavaglia recalled in a *We Out Here* magazine interview that Adele knew exactly what she was doing.

"Adele went to the BRIT school. So she's been trained on things like mic technique and has an understanding of room acoustics and reflections. Not only are her ears amazing but she also understands that there are limitations in terms of sound in each venue."

Adele once again took a busman's holiday when she stepped into the studio on two more occasions to help out with other people's songs. With Daniel Merriweather, she would handle vocal duties on the song "Water and a Flame" which would appear on the album *Love & War*. She would also reunite with old friend Jack Peñate on the song "Every Glance," which would appear on the album *Everything Is New*. The singer made a point of not publicizing what she considered fun, no-pressure gigs with friends. That she would continue to offer her services at the point when she was facing stardom spoke volumes about her character and loyalty. And the fact that, at her core, she was still just a fan of music and musicians.

Tim Van Der Kuil was a guitarist in the Daniel Merriweather band. He remembered how down-to-earth Adele could be in a conversation with *The Juice*. "One night we were playing (at The Shepherd's Bush Empire in London) when Adele turned up backstage. She was like 'Do you want a cup of tea?' and then made everyone in the band a cup of tea."

Adele did not remotely understand the behind-the-scenes machinations of the music industry and so, to a point, she was willing to take everything at face value and go along with it. But there was one thing Adele would not abide by . . . and that was doing dirt to her fans. That was exactly what she felt when she discovered that *19* was being rereleased in different countries with some additional tracks thrown in to sweeten another purchase. The singer was not above complaining to her label and her management about a situation she felt was exploiting her fans and casting her in a potentially bad light.

"I was furious when they did that on *19*," she told *G Magazine*. "I said no and they did it anyway."

Adele fumed for a bit and then moved on and, in the process, learned a valuable lesson. As much as labels value their artists, pop music is a commercial venture. It was a safe bet that XL and Columbia had no malicious intent and the rereleases did provide some legitimate extras, mainly some enticing live tracks (including, in one international edition, her entire live set from the Café Largo appearance). But this was an indication that Adele's loyalty knew no bounds and that she could be like a mother lion if she felt her fans were being slighted.

Adele had become an overnight sensation in a relatively short period of time. And as the year ended, her achievements would soon be honored.

Adele was nominated for four Grammys: Best New Artist, Record of the Year, Song of the Year, and Best Female Pop Vocal Performance. Initially, she had been cautious at the news of three nominations. After the initial shock, the news sent her running into her bathroom, where she stayed for a good hour as the impact of what she had been told sank in. Once she left the bathroom, she told the Minneapolis *StarTribune,* she was amazed that she had suddenly become part of a world that she never thought she would be a part of.

"I really didn't think that anybody would care about me until my third or fourth album," she told *The Washington Post.* "It didn't even bother me that my label thought I was a long shot. But then my publicist called and told me that I had actually received four nominations. I was screaming so loud that I had to put down the phone. Then my manager showed up at 4:30 in the morning with a bottle of champagne. I was so happy at that point that it didn't even bother me that the champagne was the same bottle I had bought him for a present."

Adele's amusement and disbelief in the announcement would reach a joking point when she told *The Telegraph,* "I was like 'what the fuck!' I was waiting for someone to come in and say 'You mug! We're only joking.'"

But once the shock and surprise had worn off, Adele became rather indifferent to getting such acknowledgment at such a tender age. She was particularly cautious in downplaying the nominations in an interview with *The Los Angeles Times.*

"A Grammy is like an Oscar," she said. "You win an Oscar when you give the performance of your life. I hope this isn't the performance of my life."

As they were often inclined to do, the British press, according to Adele, took her comments out of context and painted her as ungrateful in the wake of such an honor being given her at such a young age. Adele backtracked on her remarks and was soon back in the Grammys' good graces.

Across the pond, she received Best British Female and Best British Breakthrough Act from the prestigious BRIT Awards. When the dust settled on the Grammys, she would take home honors for Best New Artist and Best Pop Vocal Performance.

Even as she was picking up the Grammys and the BRITs, Adele was still in a fog about such honors. She had been shocked at the nominations. She was amazed that she had actually won some of the highest honors a performer could aspire to on her very first album.

Adele was so far removed from the idea of awards at that point that when she heard she had been nominated, she thought it had been a mistake. She reasoned that while the music "industry" people had heard of her, nobody in the real world, and especially the Grammy members who voted, had a clue who she was.

Adele's attitude toward the Grammys was typified by her attitude before and after the awards show. During the pre-show hoopla, Adele did a requisite amount of press, but when she was finished, she passed on all the hip pre-Grammy parties in favor of catching up on some movies she had missed. For the record, she saw the likes of *Doubt, The Wrestler,* and *Milk.* After capturing honors at the Grammys proper, she blew off the proper post-parties and an invite by the members of Coldplay to a hip after-hours gathering to grab some fast food at a local burger joint.

Adele would continue to be nonchalant about her Grammy

honors. So much so that, in keeping with the informal British rock tradition started by The Beatles and the Rolling Stones, she proudly displayed her Grammys and other assorted awards on a shelf in her bathroom. Carrying on this tradition would have a laughingly unexpected impact on her social life, as she explained to *Elle*.

"I was seeing this guy and he had no idea who I was. We never talked about music, which I thought was weird, but then I thought he was trying to make me feel comfortable by appearing to be unfazed by my success. The first time I took him to my house, he went to the toilet. When he came back out, he said 'Who the fuck are you?' It scared him and I never saw him again."

Midway through 2009, with her An Evening with Adele tour about to conclude, Adele was feeling confident and secure. So much so that when prying journalists would bring up questions about the cancellation of some of her 2008 tour dates, she finally went public with the demons that had been preying on her with a confession that appeared in *Nylon* magazine, that was quickly picked up by other sources, like Contact Music.

"I was really unhappy at home and there were a lot of family issues going on. But I got better. I stopped drinking. I was drinking far too much and that was kind of the relationship with this boy. I couldn't bear to be without him, so I was like 'I'll just cancel my stuff.' We refer to that period as my E.L.C., my Early Life Crisis. Now I'm sober. I can't believe I did that (canceled tour dates). It seems so ungrateful."

Not surprisingly, the rigors of recording, touring, and becoming a worldwide music icon were beginning to negatively impact Adele. She was missing birthdays, weddings, and the births of babies. A good many of her friends were falling by the wayside due primarily to her not being around.

Adele's career had become her reality.

Predictably, Adele's true confession was twisted and turned. She would acknowledge in an interview with *The Scotsman* that what she had said was only part of what was going on in her life.

"I couldn't find time for anything," she said. "I thought 'I need to go away and not be on another fucking plane trying to work out what I feel about all this stuff that had suddenly exploded.' I couldn't remember why I started doing music. I needed to be on my own and remember why I love what I do.

"I didn't feel like myself and I thought that was really dangerous."

And then there was the matter of writing some songs.

Adele's management and record label had been good about not pushing her regarding a follow-up album. However, Adele's own insecurity was working overtime. She was excited and nervous at the prospect of recording again, but she was also aware that she was only as good as her next record. But Adele's own internal psyche was already hard at work . . . with mixed results, as she explained in a BBC Newsbeat interview.

"I've just got to find something to write about," she said. "The first record, I was just completely in love. Now I'm just busy. I don't really want to write about working. I just don't have time for the heartache at the moment."

Maybe she did.

9.

EX TWO

A dele had just finished recording her first album. She was about to embark on an important international tour that would either make or break her career. There were professional obligations by the carload and no shortage of personal insecurities to deal with.

The last thing Adele needed to do was fall in love. But sometime between the recording of *19* and the beginning of her tour, that's exactly what she did.

"He was amazing," she told *Vogue*. "He was great. I can do things now that I never dreamed I'd be able to do."

High praise for a man who, like the inspiration for the album *19*, ultimately did her wrong. And, like the mystery cad of that album, this ex-love of Adele's life has also remained a mystery.

Beginning in 2011, rumors spread that the man who inspired *21* was actually British musician/actor Slinky Winfield. Speculation that it was Winfield reached such a state that Adele denied that she was ever involved nor would she ever be involved with a Slinky Winfield type.

Nor was she dating in a pool that seemed to offer much in the way of lasting romance. She had often been candid in saying that most of the men in her circle were aimless and did not have much going on in their lives. In all fairness, Adele's worldview at that point was shallow as well, with partying and hanging out in clubs being major elements in getting her through the days. So admittedly, prospects were limited.

Adele was introduced to this latest man by some friends during a round of promotion for *19*. That he was ten years older than Adele made no difference. To Adele, he was interesting, worldly, and, yes, quite attractive. He was an artsy, creative type who was not in the business and, as Adele would explain in *Rolling Stone*, he had come along at just the right time for her.

"Most of my life (at that point) was my career. Our relationship was kind of a side project. It made me feel real normal which, at the time, was just what I needed."

On the surface, Adele and this mystery man seemed the perfect example of opposites attracting. Whereas Adele was bubbling, outgoing, and could be quite loud and forward, by Adele's own estimation, her new beau was quiet, did not think much of show business, and was not interested in hearing much about her career. Quite simply, he liked the idea of a relationship isolated from the rest of Adele's world. And so did Adele.

It was the very things that attracted Adele to this man that turned off many of Adele's friends. He did not talk much. He was not enthusiastic about the club and music scene. Yet, the romance would blossom. Adele had found a lover who was kind, considerate, and who would not tolerate her bringing her work home with her.

"He was my soul mate," lamented Adele in an interview with The Huffington Post. "On every level we were totally right. We'd finish each other's sentences. He could just pick up on how I was feeling by the look in my eyes."

Adele was in love. So much so that she offered in an AOL Music Sessions interview that "In the beginning I would text him just about every ten seconds."

For that first year, her boyfriend opened up a whole new world for Adele. She was never one to travel much, and this man introduced her to the joys of different parts of the world. He guided her to books and to the idea of writing poetry. Adele was very much the Eliza Doolittle under the guiding hand of her mystery lover.

"Before I met him, all I was interested in was clubbing and getting drunk," she said in a *Rolling Stone* feature some years later, describing the relationship.

They lived together throughout the remainder of 2008 and into 2009. Adele would call and text him daily while on the Evening with Adele tour. But the time apart began to strain the relationship. Her lover had reportedly been drinking heavily in her absence, and while much of her hiatus from touring in September 2008 was tied to her abortive attempt at living alone, she also made it plain in the *Nylon* feature that "she was with her boyfriend who had been drinking."

Throughout the relationship, the man had remained faithful. Adele insisted that he never did anything wrong. Sadly and quite naturally, they fell out of love and, even worse, stayed together long enough to become bored with each other. They began fighting about inconsequential things. A cup of tea was known to bring on arguments. They stopped going out. The worst of it all, they stopped talking.

"We couldn't remember why we loved each other," she sadly confessed to *BlackBook* magazine. "It really upset me. I thought I was going to die because, when a relationship gets to the point of no return and you can't mend it, it's really devastating."

Making matters worse, once the Evening with Adele tour was over, the reality of having to start writing more songs in preparation for a follow-up album was beginning to manifest itself. Management knew enough of what was going on in Adele's personal life to step lightly around the question of a new album. They need not have, for the singer was keenly aware of what was required of her. And she was on the edge about weighing her deteriorating relationship and the realities of the business.

Truth be known, the people in Adele's inner circle of friends and business associates were thrilled when they learned that the relationship was on the rocks. They had taken every opportunity to avoid the couple, and when they did interact, they would notice that Adele was a very different person around him. Of course they wouldn't tell Adele that.

In the meantime, Adele continued to wallow in the sadness that is a relationship that has just about run its course.

She steadfastly continued to defend him to the end, insisting he did nothing wrong and that she was not upset with him. Without going into specifics, Adele had gone so far, in quotes cited in TwitLonger, to say that the relationship falling apart was her fault.

"I was pissed off at myself for not making it work," she said. "I didn't make it work. I should've made it work."

Despite blaming herself for the breakup, Adele would go through a two-year period, during the writing of the songs for the album *21,* when she would emotionally lash out at her former lover. However, by 2012, she had pretty much made peace with him, reportedly calling him up to hash things out, announcing that they were now good friends, and finally publicly giving him credit for much of her personal growth.

"I can do things that I never dreamed I'd be able to do if I hadn't met him," she offered in a Stuff.co.nz (New Zealand) interview. "I think I'd still be that little girl I was when I was eighteen. But it was never going to work."

And at the time of the breakup, the pain was simply too deep for Adele to let go of.

"I don't think I'll ever forgive myself for not making my relationship with him work," she told *Out* magazine. "He was the love of my life."

The final breakup was painful and tearful. Adele easily admitted that it was the lowest point in her life and, as she recalled in *People,* she did not handle it particularly well. "I basically locked myself in my house for nine months and drank four bottles of wine a night."

And the end of the relationship was made all the more difficult by the fact that Adele had to report to the recording studio the very next morning to begin work on *21.*

10

NO BALLAD, NO CRY

A dele began writing new material for her follow-up record in April 2009.

But not before she agreed to take a flyer as an actress with a guest shot on the hit television sitcom *Ugly Betty.* It seemed like a harmless diversion from all the drama and pressure in her life. She reasoned, how hard could it be to play herself?

In the episode, Betty is dancing with her husband at their wedding when the couple is suddenly interrupted by Adele. There is some harmless banter and the next thing we know Adele is up on stage singing the song "Right As Rain."

Adele realized that that kind of promotion in America was well worth the effort, but would later acknowledge in *Vogue* that the *Ugly Betty* experience cured her of any future acting aspirations. "I can't watch it. I was so uncomfortable. I am the worst actress of all time."

But Adele was thankful for the momentary respite from

her day job as singer-songwriter on the rise. And second albums could be notoriously troublesome.

Label and management, as was often the case with developing artists, were seeking to improve on *19*. They had been a bit taken aback by the description of Adele as being "old soul" even in the most positive reviews and were hinting that some more modern musical elements could not hurt. There was talk of another round of high-profile producers and the input of other songwriters.

The latter suggestion could have been a risky move. Adele had shown with *19* that she was more than a capable songwriter. Creatively, she had seemed comfortable when working with the producers on her debut album, and there had been no reports of ego-driven breakdowns. But management felt this would be a different story. They envisioned outside people taking a bigger hand in crafting these new songs and the album's overall production, making stronger suggestions in the area of lyrics and instrumentation. The recording of this pivotal album would become a truly collaborative situation.

Adele seemed comfortable, if cautious, with so many other hands in the mix. But she was assured that any creative decisions in the studio would ultimately be made by her.

"Adele was creatively comfortable in her own skin," her manager Jonathan Dickins told *Billboard*.

The logistics of recording *21* were considerable. Whereas *19* was recorded in a handful of studios in and around London, the recording of *21* would commence in London and then resume literally on the other side of the world in Southern California. No less than eleven separate studios would be involved. They were AIR Studios, Angel Studios, Eastcote Studios, Harmony Studios, Metropolis Studios, Myaudiotonic Studios, Patriot Studios, Serenity Sound, Shangri-La Studios, Sphere Studios, and Wendyhouse Productions.

For somebody who was very much a homebody, these sessions were shaping up as a true test of Adele's emotional resolve. She would literally and figuratively be on her own, albeit with a lineup of comforting contributors.

The primary producers on board to guide Adele's new music were an interesting mix. Paul Epworth had gained quite the reputation as the performer in Lomax and for production and remix work with the likes of U2, P. Diddy, Bloc Party, and Nine Inch Nails. He was considered a steady hand with solid commercial sensibilities who was well-versed in dealing with emotion and ego. If there was a hit single to be had, Epworth, on paper, seemed the go-to producer.

Adele could tell that he had the appropriate indie credits. But her initial reaction was not good. "I felt 'Well this is not going to work,'" she told *The Independent*. "But I thought I'd go and get drunk and so we went to a pub. Luckily we hit it off."

Rick Rubin had carried the tag of "most important producer" for years and was largely known for his uncanny ability to make magic with such diverse performers as Johnny Cash, The Mars Volta, Rage Against the Machine, and Neil Diamond. Rubin was well known for a pure, Zen-like approach to coaxing spectacular music from his artists and, despite his bearded man-mountain appearance, was a soft-hearted creative spirit. It went without saying that Epworth and Rubin would bring out the best in Adele.

After the completion of *21*, Adele revealed to *The Vancouver Sun* that her side project with The Raconteurs on "Many Shades Of Black" almost resulted in Jack White climbing into the producer's chair on the album.

"It almost was Jack White," she said. "We were doing a lot of collaborations after 'Many Shades Of Black.' We were going to get together in Detroit after the 2009 Grammys and finish some tracks and then it never happened. It'll happen at some point. I definitely want to follow it up."

Adele was on board with the creative suggestions being offered for her second album. She was growing weary of being cast as a tragic figure who could only write songs about her failed relationships. Adele would have no problem creating songs that were more upbeat and contemporary.

Her own emotions were a whole other matter. As her relationship with her boyfriend was in decline, Adele wrote the song "Take It All" and presented it to him. In its earliest form, "Take It All" was simple and heartfelt. Her lover did not care for it at all.

As Adele recalled it, he made some comments that led to an argument and, for all intents and purposes, ended the relationship.

It was not an auspicious beginning to the creation of the album *21*, which began production in May 2009.

Epworth, along with *19* alum Jim Abbiss (who would turn the song "Take It All" into what many would consider the centerpiece of the album) and songwriter/producer Fraser Smith, would conduct the London portion of the recording.

On the surface, Smith appeared to be the wild card on *21*'s production list. Smith was as mild mannered and unprepossessing as they come. But one need only look at his long list of both hip and mainstream credits to sense that he would mesh with Adele. At least, that's what manager Jonathan Dickins thought when he suggested to Adele that they meet.

Dickins said in a *Music Week* profile of Smith that "he was ambitious, had a great work ethic, and a great pop sensibility." Adele took Dickins' suggestion and met with Smith at his studio. They instantly hit it off and Smith was on board.

But all the star producers in the world were not going to help Adele out of her personal and emotional issues.

It was Epworth who was the first one to see Adele when she walked in that morning after she had had that final blow-up with her ex. He had sensed that there was trouble brewing the day before, when Adele and he had attempted an informal first session. What he saw was a young woman who was in quite fragile condition.

"We'd had a fuming argument the night before," Adele told *The London Sunday Times* of the previous night's row with her soon-to-be ex. "I'd been drinking. Then I went to the studio and screamed."

"Rolling In The Deep" was angry in tone, and with good reason. Prior to its creation, the mystery lover who had recently broken her heart had admonished Adele for being weak and that, without him, she would be boring, lonely, and rubbish. For Adele, "Rolling In The Deep" was her "fuck you" to her ex.

Adele recalled in a *Calgary Sun* interview that, in the

wake of the breakup, she was insisting on writing a ballad. "And he (Epworth) was like 'Absolutely not! I want to write a fierce tune.' I kept saying, 'Feel my heartbeat, Paul.' And my heartbeat became the beat of the song."

Epworth took the creative bull by the horns. In a *New York Times* interview, he would recall the creative tug-of-war that resulted in the song "Rolling In The Deep."

"I had all these chords that I thought would be perfect for her. I tried all these out for her for about two hours. She literally sat there with a pen in her hand and she just went 'I'm not feeling anything.' And then she went 'I've got this riff, this idea' and I went 'Go on then, what is it?' "

The musical evolution of what would become *21*'s signature song went through several stages during its development. The producer remembered that the piano bridges were very much a reflection of the song "Brooklyn Zoo" by ODB. But when it came to the vocals, Adele was spot-on in referencing both Cee-Lo Green and Nina Simone.

Epworth recalled that the core of the song, verses, and basic structure were hashed out in fifteen minutes. Two hours later, a very raw but presentable "Rolling In The Deep" was completed.

With this promising start, some preliminary sessions were attempted. But when inspiration seemed in short supply, the sessions for *21* were canceled and Adele went into seclusion. Where, for a time, she wrote, often with a drink or more in her, and contemplated the end of the relationship and that, despite not wanting to repeat with an album of "bad relationship" songs, her focus was on the man she had loved and lost and it was inevitably finding its way into the lyrics of songs she began writing.

Adele chronicled the dark days in a conversation with America's *People* when she explained, "I was really angry, then I was really bitter, then I was really lonely, then I was devastated."

"I told everybody I knew not to call me for six months," she told *BlackBook* magazine. "But in a few days it was like 'What am I meant to be doing?' I actually forgot about the last album. Nobody was putting pressure on me because they knew if they did, I wouldn't deliver."

Reports began to surface during Adele's self-imposed isolation that she was quietly dating again. But if she was, these attempts at seeing other people were so fleeting that the press chose not to pursue them. Adele would neither confirm or deny the reports.

By early 2010, Adele had indeed delivered a series of completed songs, fragments of lyrics, and a lot of ideas for the songs that would appear on the album.

Adele's world was reduced to going to the studio in the morning and going home, walking her dog, and writing at night. But, as she recalled in an interview with MSN Music, she made a concerted effort to "just swim in music."

"I literally just sat in my house and just listened to loads of music. Loads of hip-hop, loads of country, loads of pop; stuff I liked already and stuff I did not like. I was just trying to understand what it was about a song that moved me."

Once her creative instincts kicked in, *21* was out of the blocks and moving steadily forward.

As the songwriting and subsequent recording progressed, Adele brought a new element into creative play. She recalled that while on tour in support of *19*, she got an introduction to country music.

"We were on the bus doing the American tour," she recalled in a Country Music Television interview. "I used to smoke at the front of the bus and the driver would be up there driving and listening to this incredible music that I'd never heard. He could see the look on my face, I was like a child. I would say 'Who's this?' and he would say 'Garth Brooks' and I would say 'Who's Garth Brooks?' and he would bust out laughing."

The bus driver was happy to educate the young singer. He began making country music compilation tapes for Adele and, under the informal guidance of the bus driver, Adele learned to listen to and appreciate classic country crooners like Johnny Cash, Dolly Parton, Loretta Lynn, and The Carter Family. Word soon got around that Adele had gone country, and her tour manager and others were offering up their own tapes, which included some of the more modern practitioners like Alison Krauss, Rascal Flatts, Lady Antebellum, and, yes, Garth Brooks. What the singer quickly latched on to was the simplicity of the music and the stories they told.

"It's not fussy," she told CMT. "It's not trying to be trendy or clever. It's just stories and that, to me, is what music is about."

It seemed like the perfect adjunct to her soul and blues vocals, and more than a few hints of country would eventually make their way onto the album.

The song "Set Fire To The Rain" was typical of the spontaneous, truly magical moments that would populate *21*. Long a fan of Fraser T. Smith's work, in particular his credits with James Morrison and Cee-Lo Green, Adele had jumped at the chance to work with him. And Smith's triple-threat instincts—producer, songwriter, and engineer—were very much in play the day Adele walked into the session.

"When she walked into the session, I already had a rolling drumbeat going and some chords in my head," he told *M*. "She delivered a great vocal and we bashed it out in a couple of hours."

Originally the final version of "Set Fire To The Rain" was supposed to be produced by Rick Rubin. But when everybody heard how great Adele's vocals were on the demo, the only additions that were made were a drum track and string arrangements.

Sporadic dustups between Adele and her ex would continue during the recording of *21* and would lead to a musical marriage between Adele and musician/producer Ryan Tedder (OneRepublic) that would result in the song "Turning Tables." Adele had met Tedder during the 2009 Grammys. They hit it off during a laughable elevator ride in which they attempted a conversation through a handful of balloons Adele was holding. Tedder expressed an interest in collaborating with the singer on upcoming songs. Tedder had a reputation for being meticulous in the studio while also being an outside-the-box thinker. Adele readily agreed to the offer, and when the sessions for *21* began, she rang him up.

Tedder was thrilled but, admittedly, somewhat in the dark regarding Adele's musical vibe. And so after a crash course with *19*, he arrived at the studio on the appointed day four hours early in an attempt to work out chord and voice shadings that would be appropriate for the singer. After three hours, Tedder gave up in frustration and, as he told *M*, "I said 'to hell with this,' I'm going to write something that I want to hear. So I came up with an opening piano sequence and a couple of lyrics. Then Adele walked in."

Tedder explained the idea behind the bare bones of "Turning Tables." He had not known about Adele's latest fight with her ex, and so he was amazed when the singer said that the sentiment of what he had presented was exactly what was going on with her. Adele and Tedder began the process of firing ideas and lyrics at each other. Given Adele's emotional state at the moment, the rest of the song's lyrics came thick and fast. The demo for "Turning Tables" would be finished in a few hours over two days. Veteran Adele producer Abiss would ultimately head up production on the final version of "Turning Tables."

With a good half of *21* now in the can, it was time for Adele to relocate to Malibu, California, where Rick Rubin would produce another half-dozen cuts. Adele was not what you would call a summer-at-the-beach kind of girl. Consequently, her days at Mailbu were marked by heat rash, sunburn, and blisters. But the physical discomfort was more than made up for by the opportunity to record with Rubin.

Adele had been a fan of Rubin and his work for years. When the Rubin-produced *Californication* by the Red Hot Chili Peppers came out, fifteen-year-old Adele was mesmerized. Their paths crossed briefly during her *Saturday Night Live* appearance, in which Rubin was also a guest. But it remained for the Hollywood Bowl appearance that ended her *19* tour to cement their creative relationship.

"He came up and said 'You're so different live. You've got to get your live show across on record,'" she related in an interview with the *Calgary Sun*. "I felt like going 'Do you want to do it Rick?' But I was like 'I can't say that to Rick Rubin.' He'd be like 'Do you know who I am?'" But I tried to mentally plant the seed."

It was a seed that would take root after Adele captured Best New Artist honors at the 2009 Grammys.

Prior to the Grammy Awards, Adele attended the posh charity party, MusiCares. As part of the party's festivities, some of the biggest names in the business were invited to sing. Although considered by many to be the new kid on the block, Adele readily accepted the invitation. Adele told *Clash* magazine what happened next.

"I sang there and I was actually the worst of the night," she remembered. "I followed Jennifer Hudson and I just know I was shit. Rick came up to me afterwards and tried to boost my confidence by saying 'It was brilliant, it was great.' Later that night, after I had won Best New Artist, Rick e-mailed me and said, 'Shall we do a record together?'"

Adele penciled in April 2010 for a five-week stint at Rubin's Malibu studio. That much was set in stone. But *21* had quickly evolved into a naturalistic and quite emotional project. Adele's emotional state, rather than a stumbling block, had become quite the catalyst for outside collaborations and spontaneous creation during the London phase of the recording. There was no reason to believe that process would not continue in the States.

At the suggestion of Columbia Records Group president Ashley Newton, Adele agreed to meet with songwriter Greg Wells to work out something that was not on Adele's song list for Rubin. As a producer/songwriter/player, Wells had worked with a lot of people Adele had admired, such as Mika, Katy Perry, and Pink. As she walked into Wells' Culver City, California, studio, she felt possibilities.

Wells was clearly starstruck by Adele, as he explained in an *American Songwriter* interview. "To have her singing her ideas sounding the way she sounds, it's kind of spoiled me forever."

In a video interview on her Web site, Adele looked back on the idea that the song "One And Only" would run contrary to the tone of much of the album. "The song is not about the same guy that the record is about. It's about somebody I've known for years. We've always liked each other but we've never really been together. It's more a song of intention."

The songwriting process was fairly simple. Wells started out playing a slow piano progression. Across the room, Adele was pacing, her ever-present pad and pen at hand. Wells told *American Songwriter* what happened next.

"Finally she said, 'I'm not sure if this is good, but what do you think of this?' And then in full voice she sang the finished chorus of 'One And Only' and I almost fell over."

The collaboration lasted three days and, after a slight tweak by songwriter Dan Wilson, "One And Only" was added to an ever-growing list of potential cuts for *21*.

The song "Rumor Has It" played fast and loose with the

album's overall theme of love lost and betrayal. And it was the first time that Adele directly addressed the alleged rumors close friends had spread as a contributing factor to the breakup.

During her L.A. stay, Adele also reconnected with Ryan Tedder and turned his notion of a bluesy-*cum*-Radiohead vibe into the basis for the song "Rumor Has It." Adele's collaborator continued to be bowled over by the ease and speed in which the singer plied her craft. Typically a four- or five-hour job to record vocals, Adele did a pitch-perfect run-through of "Rumor Has It" in ten minutes.

"Rumor Has It" was a particularly thorny issue for Adele. The song was in response to the fact that she discovered close friends had been gossiping about her and that these bits of rumor and gossip always seemed to be making their way into the tabloid papers and Internet blogs. To test her theory, Adele went so far as to make up stories, feed them to certain friends, and watch as these falsehoods made the rounds in order to determine who had spread the rumors.

"It's about my own friends believing the stuff they hear about me," she explained to Digital Spy. "It's all pretty mortifying."

After completing sessions in Los Angeles, it was up to Malibu, where Adele was about to experience a different kind of recording process.

Rick Rubin had always been a contrary sort when it came to producing: quick to fly in the face of prevailing attitudes and, in the case of Adele, insisting on a very live recording situation. To that extent, he said, no music samples or electronic instruments would be used. He brought in a live band of musicians, who would add to the spontaneous nature of the sessions.

Rubin had a near-encyclopedic knowledge of musicians and instinctively knew which ones would easily adjust to the recording process he had in mind. The band would be made up of the seasoned professionals Chris Dave (drums), Matt Sweeney (guitar), James Poyser (piano), and Pino Palladino (bass).

Adele admitted to being unsure about this progressive approach.

"I didn't think we would fit in together at all," she told *Clash*. "That's why I was so intrigued to do it. I think it was a challenge for both of us and I think that's why we wanted to do it."

Rubin had the reputation as being an easygoing yet notorious control freak. Adele was initially unsure about how sessions with essentially no structure and lots of improvisation would sit with her. But she admitted in a widely circulated YouTube video interview that she "was coming from a braver place" after the spontaneity of the London sessions and so was more than willing to test the waters of Rubin's brave new world.

Rubin's live band approach to recording had presented Adele's recording environment in almost surreal terms. Adele would offer in several post-recording interviews that recording under those conditions presented an insulated, timeless quality to the process.

"It was all about the songs, all about the music," she told MSN Music. "We just vibed until it felt right."

But she would admit to *Q* that there were those first-day jitters. She was feeling homesick and missing her mother. She was alone in the States and not totally secure in the working situation—all of which combined to make her first day in Malibu a rough one.

"The first day I had a breakdown. I lost it and started crying and had to go for a walk on the beach to sort myself out. After that I was fine, though I still had the odd moment."

Rubin was understanding and patient. It was not the first time a singer had a moment of doubt on his watch, which is why he knew Adele would come out of it.

Adele held it together enough to get into the flow of how this new phase of recording would work. While there would be endless takes, more often than not Adele's first or second vocal run-through would be the one selected for the song. Her diligence and focus were drawing praise from the producers and musicians as well as the equally impressed behind-the-scenes people.

Sound mixer Tom Elmhirst had been down the recording road with Adele on her first album and, as he explained to *Sound on Sound*, he returned because of her musical character. "I had already mixed some of the material on Adele's first album and knew what she was all about. She's someone who breaks the mold."

During the sessions, Adele would find the time to truly exercise her new country influence with the song "Don't You Remember," which she would write during the Malibu recording sessions.

"What gave me the courage to try and do that ('Don't You Remember') was the country song 'Need To Know,'" she told CMT. "It was everywhere. I couldn't change the channel on the radio without hearing that song. You couldn't escape it but, luckily I loved it. The feeling that song gave me, I was trying to channel that into my own song."

Adele also managed to exercise her newfound love for the bluegrass band The Steeldrivers when she recorded their song "If It Hadn't Been For Love." The banjo-flavored song would not ultimately make the final cut of the album but would appear as a bonus track on a later edition of *21* and would be a crowd-pleaser in many of her live performances.

Throughout the sessions that produced the songs "Don't You Remember," "He Won't Go" (a radical thematic departure dedicated to a friend who was addicted to heroin), the final pass on "One And Only," "I Found A Boy," and the cover of INXS' "Never Tear Us Apart," Rubin was gentle but firm, encouraging his charges to take every element of every song that extra step. Rubin would later acknowledge that the emphasis on more spontaneity and less restraint would produce pleasant surprises on a daily basis.

One such surprise came on the day that Rubin and Adele decided to scrap "Never Tear Us Apart" in favor of a spur-of-the-moment live workout on a song that hit very close to home for Adele, The Cure's "Lovesong," a song that Rubin had long coveted as something Barbra Streisand might be interested in.

For Adele, the decision to record "Lovesong" could not have come at a better time. As the sessions were winding down, Adele was finding herself increasingly homesick for her mother and friends, and the song was a nostalgic nod to the first concert she had attended with her mother and how The Cure had been a major influence in her life over the years.

"Her singing was strong and powerful in the studio," the producer told *M* of the "Lovesong" session. "It was clear something very special was happening. The musicians were inspired, as they rarely get to play with the artist present. This was truly a magic moment. None of the musicians knew exactly what they were going to play and were listening so deeply to Adele to see where they fit in."

Rubin would later assess the "Lovesong" session when he said everybody in the studio was reduced to tears. And those would not be the last tears shed during the *21* sessions.

Recording an album with such a constant and very high emotional tone can be rough. For Adele, there were continuous takes that stretched her vocal powers to the limits. For the band, there was the constant challenge of playing and improvising on command. It was safe to say that, emotionally, everybody involved in the sessions was walking a tightrope.

After the demo for "Set Fire To The Rain" was completed, Smith was under the impression that Rubin would do the final production and that his work on *21* was done.

"I didn't hear from Adele because she was in Malibu recording," he told *Music Life*. "But when she got back to London, she asked me to come to her flat and she played me the version that Rick had done. It was great and it was completely different from what we had done on the demo. But I think we both felt that the demo was the nucleus of what the song should be."

Smith's solution was to record live drum tracks, add a string arrangement and, after two days of attempting to rere-cord the vocals, Adele and Smith agreed that the original vo-cal track on the demo was what ultimately set the proper tone.

Adele had nothing but praise for the Rubin sessions and the nurturing vibe he had created in the studio. But she was candid in an interview that appeared in Pressparty and nu-merous outlets that she had been uncomfortable with the lifestyle of the rich and famous that made up the Malibu colony.

"I'm a London girl through and through," she said. "I felt very uncomfortable in Malibu. It's not my kind of area. Everybody is rich and they live behind these gates. Every-body drives. I thought I would walk to a cute little water-front café and hang out. But you can't walk anywhere."

As the sessions for *21* were winding down, Adele heard from a mutual friend that her ex-lover had recently an-nounced his engagement to another woman. Adele told *New York Post.com* that she was "devastated" at the news. But she made the decision that she did not want to grow old with all the anger and disappointment from the relationship that had fueled the fire of *21*.

"I thought this guy needs to be shown in a good light. He was the love of my life and now it was over."

Adele went with the moment, sat down, and in ten min-utes had written the bulk of the lyrics that would become "Someone Like You."

The suggestion that yet another song be thrown into the mix that was essentially full to overflowing did not faze anybody.

In fact producer Rubin and others connected to the label encouraged Adele to get together with singer-songwriter Dan Wilson to see what they could come up with.

Wilson, the former lead singer of the group Semisonic, had gone on to become the "first call" writer to the stars, collaborating with the likes of Josh Groban, John Legend, Faith Hill, and Keith Urban. The fact that he was in Semisonic proved the icebreaker when Adele and he met for the first time.

"The first time we met, she told me, 'My mum wanted to make sure that I told you that she's a big fan of Semisonic,'" he related to the *StarTribune*. "We had a good laugh about that."

After they stopped laughing, they got down to business with Adele telling him that the basis of this song-to-be was her recent terrible breakup.

Wilson recalled in *PopMatters* that a new song at that point would be under a deadline situation and that Adele and he would have a matter of days to put something together for a listening session in Malibu. He also remembered that his marching orders from producer Rubin were vague. "I asked Rick Rubin what kind of thing he was looking for. He said, 'We're just looking for a great song.' So I didn't really have any preconceptions."

Adele took Rubin's advice and asked Wilson to help her give form to what, at that point, were the skeletal outlines of the song. The songwriter was not going in blindly. He was a legitimate fan of Adele's and songs from *19* were regular listens on his iPod.

Wilson recalled what happened next in a conversation

with the *LA Weekly*. "She had at least four lines when we got together. While we worked on it, what became clear was that this was somebody who—years had gone by and she still couldn't let go of the love she felt."

To get in the proper mood for fleshing out the song, Wilson and Adele listened to a number of Wanda Jackson tunes to catch the down-and-dirty kind of vibe that the singer was looking for.

But, as chronicled in an interview with the Web site Weeping Elvis, the process by which "Someone Like You" came into being had its tense moments.

"We didn't have any arguments or tussles," said Wilson in an *American Songwriter* interview. "There may have been some points where I suggested that a certain line might be better. But on this one, Adele knew exactly what she wanted to say."

And what Adele wanted to say was nothing if not direct.

"She never told me this directly but I think she felt that she could do something less metaphorical with me," he said in the Weeping Elvis piece. "Something less about wordplay and more about telling the story and being emotional and strong in a very vulnerable way."

Two-thirds of the song was completed by the end of the first day. It was far from complete but, when they stopped for the day, they both felt they were on the right track. Little did Wilson know that a surprise would be waiting for him when the pair met up the next day. Unbeknownst to Wilson, Adele had taken the very rough and incomplete tapes and played them for both her mother and her manager. Wilson recalled being a bit perturbed at the news.

"I said, 'It's not finished. Why did you do that?' It scared me. Then I asked her what they thought of it. Adele said her manager loved it and her mother cried. That was with big blank areas, no lyrics in the second verse, and the bridge wasn't written."

The pair set about finishing the song. Lyrics were reworked to Adele's satisfaction and the bridge was written between Adele's hourly cigarette breaks. They would also end up rerecording portions of the vocal track when it was found that Adele's second-day vocals had a more appropriate desperate quality to them.

Adele would later jokingly tell friends that Wilson was a slave driver during their sessions, but would then offer that, in the most positive manner, the songwriter had worked her harder than she had ever worked before.

"Dan brought out the soppy side of me," she told *The Advertiser*. "Before that, I was just writing bitter, angry songs."

A very basic demo of "Someone Like You" was recorded, Adele's heart-wrenching vocals over a simple piano backing. At the end of the second day, Adele went up to Malibu to play the demo for Rubin and some label people. Wilson heard nothing for a few months. Then he started getting reports that everybody who had heard the demo had cried. Wilson knew that in the songwriting business, if people cried it was a good sign.

Originally the demo was something that was going to be filed away for future consideration. When it suddenly became a contender for inclusion in *21*, Wilson recalled in *American Songwriter*, "My initial impression was that they were going to add strings and a choir and turn it into a Chrissie Hynde power ballad."

But the emotions the song wrought in Adele literally forced her to essentially make a slightly tweaked version of the demo of "Someone Like You" the very last song on *21*. The album was now officially done

And Adele was now truly free.

11

21 TO LIFE

n the eve of the release of *21*, Adele spent the evening out on the town with a small circle of friends. But at the end of the night, and mere minutes from the official *21* drop, Adele was home with her mother and, as she told *Billboard*, much more relaxed than she had been during the countdown to the release of the album *19*.

"Everything is less frantic than it was the first time around," she said. "I've learned to sit down and enjoy it all. I feel more free than I ever have."

Adele was not alone in implying personal as well as professional growth. Those in her inner circle were most likely noticing the little things that showed she had matured. The sense of swagger and confidence that she now projected was miles removed from the tentative nature of the previous years. By degrees, she was more definitive in her decisions and had, through the largely collaborative nature of *21*, learned some important creative lessons about working with others and still maintaining her integrity and creative vision. Adele was only twenty-one, but she was no longer a little girl.

Adele's second album was completed in May 2010. Everybody on the business side of the singer's career was thrilled with the results. But that did not mean there would not be changes.

Originally the album was going to take its title from the song "Rolling In The Deep." But Adele decided that *21* would be a better title because, like its predecessor *19,* that was the year this follow-up had been recorded, and the growth she had experienced as a performer truly represented her coming of age at twenty-one. But she would jokingly concede that the days of her album titles being her age were now in the past.

Then there was the matter of when to release the album. Initially a November 2010 release had been slated, all the better to capture the Christmas holiday buyers and to keep her release of new material within the two-year period most labels preferred. However, Columbia was so enthused with the album that they begged for and received some extra time to roll out a massive marketing campaign in the States that would target everybody who had bought her previous album, increase her all-important Internet presence, and hook her up with selected press for prerelease interviews.

Spoken in hushed tones was concern about whether Adele was still a relevant artist after a two-year interlude or if *19* had simply been a product of timing and luck. The consensus among those in the business side of things was that she most definitely was more than a one-hit wonder.

But there was also some concern that, perhaps, Adele had come too late to the party when it came to young female singer-songwriters. Despite her obvious credentials, Amy Winehouse's nonmusic antics were tarnishing her obvious genius. Duffy and other members of the BRIT School generation were having moderate success but nothing that was truly consistent. And the reality was that while the more garish and theatrical rock and pop acts like Lady Gaga were critically dismissed at every opportunity, their records continued to go multiplatinum and gold. By comparison, Adele was the critics' darling but even her most ardent supporters had to admit that with only one album to date and another on the horizon, there were still many questions that needed to be answered. *21* would be the record to either make or break Adele.

In December, Adele continued to show how country had become a part of her life when she recorded a live duet with country star Darius Rucker of Lady Antebellum's "Need To Know" during Country Music Television's *Artists of the Year* special. That song, along with live acoustic versions of "Someone Like You," "Turning Tables," and "Don't You Remember," would appear on a Target special edition two-CD disc of *21*.

Adele's willingness to branch out into different musical genres and to take chances was noted. The *Village Voice*, in a preview/review/analysis of the prospects for Adele's *21*, made a point of saying that Adele had gotten to the stage where her music was something that both Patti Smith and Linkin Park could relate to. The piece also indicated that it went without saying that Adele was making friends with her conversion to country and bluegrass.

But behind all the happy talk and positive vibes, there was still some concern about how well *21* would ultimately fare. If the album did what *19* had accomplished, the bean counters would be thrilled. But "if" is a mighty imposing word, and nobody had their fingers crossed tighter than Adele.

"I don't think this record will do anything," she confessed to *Entertainment Weekly*. "I can't feel the buzz in America."

Columbia Records CEO Rob Stringer was cautiously optimistic in *EW*: "When everybody heard the record they knew it was special. But not one person could honestly tell you they thought it would sell that many (albums)."

To that end, Adele was once again on the prerelease promotion trail in America. And a good part of that promotion was centered in the seemingly unlikely halls of Target and Best Buy. To many, making nice to the bastions of middle-class consumerism seemed very unhip and even hinted at sellout. Adele was quick to defend her courting of retail America in a conversation with the *Illinois Entertainer*.

"Target did quite well by me on the first record so of course I was going to see them," she said. "And I saw both of them (Target and Best Buy) at separate meetings, which meant flying around in this real tiny plane. And I'm not real big on flying."

Adele explained to *IE* with no small amount of sincerity that doing a concert for the Target bigwigs was a gas. "The first time I went on the first record in front of Target, there were maybe four people. This time I was in a five-hundred-capacity room and a thousand people turned up. They were all cheering and whooping. It was crazy."

Best Buy would go equally well, and the consensus from the stores that were known to satisfy the steady diet of Midwest music buyers was that the sooner Columbia could get *21* into their hands the better.

After some discussion, it was agreed that *21* would make its debut in January 2011.

But it was also important to the ultimate success of *21* that at least one single make an appearance before year's end and so, in November 2010, "Rolling In The Deep" made its debut at No. 2 on the UK singles charts, right behind Bruno Mars' song "Grenade." Adele's song would remain at No. 2 for four weeks and in the Top 10 for ten weeks.

"Rolling In The Deep" seemed the perfect first single to hit the airwaves. It was powerful in that low-down confessional way that had quickly become Adele's trademark. The instrumental backing was blues and soul done up in a raw pop fashion. The song showed how Adele had grown, and gave a hint of what fans could look forward to. Adele agreed with the choice of "Rolling In The Deep" as the ideal first single out of the chute. She sensed that the song would be something special.

In December 2010, the song made its debut on the US Billboard charts at a surprising No. 68. But like its predecessors, "Rolling In The Deep" would eventually make it to No. 1. Many saw the success of "Rolling In The Deep" as the benchmark, the missing piece to the puzzle that would make Adele a major star in America. Now it was simply a matter of getting the singer back on the road and in front of the masses.

And to, hopefully, avoid the pitfalls that plagued portions of the Evening with Adele tour. Adele did not appear to have any emotional entanglements that could disrupt a tour this time around. She was healthy. To a large extent she had gotten her homesickness and stage fright under control. Even her long-standing fear of flying had improved. Adele was pronounced fit to travel.

A tour in support of *21* was in its preliminary stage. Ever the perfectionist, Adele reasoned that adding a second guitarist to her backing band would give her live sound more depth as she gradually moved up to larger-scale clubs and concert halls. She immediately thought of Van Der Kuil from the Daniel Merriweather days and advised her management to track him down and add him to the band.

In turn, Van Der Kuil was able to point Adele in the direction of a quite-capable bassist in Australian Sam Dixon. Dixon, who also included songwriting and production credits on his résumé, had been around a while, seen it all, and was not easily impressed. But the musician was exactly that, as he explained in a conversation with CanCulture.

"She is incredibly heartfelt and honest at all times," he said. "She is not a diva."

Backup singer Kelli-Leigh Henry-Davila joined the Adele touring band around the time of *21*'s release and, like Dixon, found her new employer extremely down-to-earth. "She was always, 'Can I make you some tea?'" she explained to a BBC News reporter. "There was no diva in her."

By the time *21* made its initial chart appearances, Adele had already spent some time on the international promotion trail. Always a trooper when it came to promoting her music, she never tired of talking up *21,* and early reviews indicated that there was much to talk about. Her personal life as it pertained to the nature of the songs once again were open to discussion, but press interest also centered on the maturity of the sound compared to *19* and, in particular, the infusion of country and roots music into her already-established soul and blues elements.

When she was not doing interviews, Adele was more than happy to perform. Adele made musical appearances on December 9, 2010, at the Royal Variety Performance; on the finale of Holland's singing competition show, *The Voice of Holland*, on January 21, 2011; and on BBC 1's *Live Lounge* on January 27. The week *21* was released in the UK, Adele performed a short acoustic set of *21* songs at London's Tabernacle music hall that was simultaneously broadcast live on her official Web site.

It was during the Paris phase of the promotional tour that a singer's worst nightmare hit Adele. While performing as part of a Paris radio station promo segment, Adele's voice suddenly went from her trademark contralto to a rough, raw, barely audible rasp and finally to a whisper. Adele had dealt with sore throats and colds over the years, but as she recalled in an interview with *Vogue*, this was something different.

"That day it (my voice) just went. It was literally like someone had pulled a curtain over it."

Dixon told *The West Australian* that he was not surprised that her voice gave out. "She never doesn't give 100 percent. Even at a six a.m. radio promo she's still at the top of her game. That's the reason why I think she's ended up crook (with voice problems). Even at a sound check she'll be singing at her absolute maximum."

It did not help matters that compressed schedules would

often have her doing a late-night promo appearance, get very little sleep, and then get up early the next morning for another promo and another song. Whether anybody cared to admit it, Adele was willingly burning the candle at both ends and her body was beginning to bog down.

Adele flew back to London the next day and consulted with her doctor, who diagnosed the singer with acute laryngitis. After a couple of weeks' rest, her voice returned and Adele returned to the promo trail without missing a beat.

But it was an early sign that Adele and those around her would have to begin paying closer attention to her health, which would mean a modification of her singing duties. She would no longer sing for radio promotion appearances and, while they knew it was an impossible task, Adele's people would insist that she only sing at half strength during sound checks to rest her voice for shows.

While Adele grudgingly went along with the suggestions, her youthful enthusiasm and sense of invincibility would often prevail over prudence. Adele most likely felt she knew her body better than anyone else. And that her body told her she was fine.

During this period, Adele was also not neglecting the States, recalling how much more difficult it had been to break *19*. And she would be a good sport about even the most questionable promotional events. In October, Adele performed a short set and did a meet and greet with two hundred executives from the Target retail chain, which would pay it forward with a massive push behind a live version of *21* that would be released in 2011. That same month, she flew to Los Angeles where she did a set for some local and national tastemakers at the Largo.

In advance of the release of *21* in the States, Adele also did a February 2011 blitz of the daytime and nighttime talk show circuit, appearing on *The Jay Leno Show, The David Letterman Show, Today, The Ellen DeGeneres Show,* and *Jimmy Kimmel Live!* During the month of February, Adele also made her motion picture sound track debut when it was announced that "Rolling In The Deep" would appear on the sound track for the science fiction action movie *I Am Number Four.*

While back in London, Adele appeared at the 2011 BRIT Awards. It was a different time for her. She was home and now a full-fledged star, a mere two years removed from obscurity. It would be a very emotion-filled night that would include her live performance of the song "Someone Like You." Adele was probably more than a bit nervous this night as the inspiration for the song, the loss of an ex-lover, was suddenly once again fresh in her mind.

Adele would later admit that while singing the song that night, she could envision her former lover and imagine his gloating over the power he still had over her. Which is why, as she neared the end of her performance, tears welled up in her eyes and she broke down.

Adele would later explain the public breakdown in an interview with ITV2. "I was really emotional by the end because I'm quite overwhelmed by everything anyway. And then I had a vision of my ex, of him watching me at home, and he's going to be laughing at me because he knows I'm crying because of him, with him thinking, 'Yes, she's still wrapped around my finger.'"

Band member Dixon had experienced these emotional moments several times during his tenure with the band and acknowledged to CanCulture that "There are some nights where she can really be affected by what she's singing and we as a band have to be aware of that."

Adele had developed a particularly good taste for the States on her *19* tour, and that continued the second time around. When she was not making small talk and often-mindless banter with her TV hosts, she managed a bit of the nightlife, especially in New York and Los Angeles, and speculated on how she might move to New York at some point in the future.

But the immediate concern was how successful *21* would be. And amid a rush of positive reviews, Adele's sophomore effort was a smash right out of the box.

In the UK, *21* was smashing long-held sales records seemingly every day. *21* debuted at No. 1 on the UK album charts on January 30, 2011, and, in the process, dragged her previous album, *19*, back to the top of the charts at No. 4. When the single "Someone Like You" jumped an amazing forty-six spots from No. 47 to No. 1, and the follow-up, "Rolling In The Deep," followed to No. 4, Adele became the first performer since The Beatles in 1964, to have two albums and two singles in the Top 5 simultaneously, a feat that would land Adele in *The Guinness Book Of World Records* by year's end. Shortly thereafter when *19*, after 102 weeks on the album charts, rose to No. 2, Adele added another world record, becoming the first artist since The Corrs in 1999 to hold the top two album slots.

As with the previous album, critics were lining up to sing Adele's praises.

The *Village Voice* said, "The album has a diva's stride and a diva's purpose. With a touch of sass and lots of grandeur, it is often a magical thing."

The *Chicago Tribune* stated that the album "Beefs up the rhythmic drive and the drama of the arrangements."

Music OMH remarked, "*21* is one of the great breakup records and the first truly impressive record of 2011."

The longevity of *21* would be reflected in three separate stints as the No. 1 album, for a total of eighteen weeks between February and July 2011. As almost an afterthought, the album would top the charts in a total of twenty-six countries by year's end.

No less amazing was the success of *21* in America. The album debuted on February 22, 2011, at the top of the Billboard charts. The album would remain in the Top 3 for twenty-three consecutive weeks and in the Top 5 for thirty-nine consecutive weeks.

Flushed with the success of the album, and while at least a year away from considering a third album, Adele told *Q* magazine that she was already looking to the future.

She joked that the next album would probably be called *23, 26,* or *27.* But she was quite serious that the follow-up would be done her way.

"It won't be a big production. I want it to be quite acoustic and piano led. I want to write it, record it, produce it, and master it on my own. When I move into my new house, which will probably be this summer (2011), my sound engineer is going to come over and help me install a studio and teach me how to use it."

But Adele would have to push those plans back as the inevitable world tour in support of *21* was quickly rounding into shape. With the rocky way in which the *19* tour played out still fresh in her head, Adele felt that this time everything had to be flawless. She was looking forward to the tour and, as she told *Billboard*, she was prepared for the emotional stresses that would be there with her on stage every night.

"Towards the end of touring on *19*, there were a couple of shows where I'd be singing 'Make You Feel My Love' and I would just have to start thinking of Ikea or something.

"You just have to switch off sometimes."

12

LIGHTS … CAMERA

Adele seemed a natural when it came to the expected run of music videos that would accompany her songs. She was herself, quietly animated and at ease in front of the camera. Equally important was that the songs projected a nuanced, almost noir tone about them that would result in quite inventive storytelling.

In keeping with the tone of the projected videos, Adele and her management cast a fairly wide and hip net, and the result would be a highly imaginative group of filmmakers.

CHASING PAVEMENTS

Adele said the storyline for her "Chasing Pavements" video was pretty literal. "I had a shit boyfriend who I knew would be shit," she explained to Spyder's Random Things. "I knew when I got with him that it would be a car-crash relationship."

Hence the car-crash story line in which Adele is pictured from two different perspectives in a car crash: one in which she lays inside the wreckage before climbing out to observe the other accident victims being taken away by ambulance. The second element of the video shows Adele and her ex recovering from a breakup and rekindling their passion in the moments leading up to the crash. As this element plays out, we see Adele and her lover motionless on the ground as they are taken away. It is all very dark, effectively theatrical and, by visual turns, very surreal.

Director Mathew Cullen had already made quite a name for himself in the music video world on the strength of videos for the groups Weezer, R.E.M., Beck, and Modest Mouse.

Cullen had been trying forever to get a job with XL. "Finally we got the track from Adele," he said in an interview with Anatomy of a Music Video. "She knew our work and she was a fan so it was a natural collaboration."

Set in London but filmed in Los Angeles, Cullen recalled that his marching orders were to be "creatively ambitious." But the fact that "Chasing Pavements" would be Adele's first video also weighed heavily on his approach.

"When I listened to the song, I was inspired by the idea of following after someone you love even though it will never work out," he explained to AOAMV. "The unconscious couple coming to life to retell the story of their relationship was a perfect storytelling device for the themes."

Adele acquitted herself quite well in front of the camera, fully natural in the dramatic and romantic sequences and more than capable of conveying the eerie and surreal nature of the piece.

COLD SHOULDER

Easily the most bizarre Adele video to date, "Cold Shoulder" had the odd distinction of being directed by Phil Griffin who, in his day job, is the president of the cable news channel MSNBC.

Filmed in London, the atmospheric, stark video opens with Adele sitting in a darkened room surrounded by the faces of melting ice statues whose expressions are of extreme despair. At the conclusion of the video, Adele's face melds into the faces of the melting ice sculptures. Creepy stuff by anybody's standards, "Cold Shoulder" received massive exposure upon its release and many favorable reviews that said the video captured the essence of the song.

From an acting point of view, Adele was challenged in the solitude and underlying hopelessness of it all but managed the introspective nature of the video quite well, proving that, despite her early movie and television bits, she could be a believable actress in certain contexts.

HOMETOWN GLORY

There was no official video the first time "Hometown Glory" made its recorded debut as a limited-edition single in 2007, although several YouTube performance videos would quickly hit the Internet. It would remain for the song's official release a year later to finally generate a proper, polished video. XL chose veteran director Paul Dugdale to fashion the "Hometown Glory" piece. Dugdale was a seasoned director of films, television, awards shows and, of late, videos by the likes of The Prodigy and Cajun Dance Party. He knew his way around elements of starkness and fantasy, both of which would come into play in the "Hometown Glory" video.

A London parking structure served as the backdrop for the desolate and quite haunting visage of Adele, alone with her thoughts and a contemplative piano backup, singing as a series of posters depicting cities revolves around her with dramatic regularity: a simple yet quite effective visual treatment that nailed the intent of the song.

MAKE YOU FEEL MY LOVE

By the time Adele had decided to do her first cover, the Bob Dylan–penned "Make You Feel My Love," the song had already gone through the hands of Billy Joel, Garth Brooks, Joan Osborne, and countless others. When it came to Adele's video, the consensus was that a mixture of then and now would be appropriate.

Enter director Matt Kirkby, a veteran of the Ridley Scott school of filmmaking who had cut his teeth on numerous commercials and music videos for Basement Jaxx, Muse, and Jamiroquai. The director came up with a story line that examined the dichotomy of longing and modern technology.

The premise was fairly straightforward: Adele is sitting alone in a darkened room at four in the morning. She is missing a relationship she feels is over and, as she sings, she is texting the mystery man in hopes of salvaging the relationship. In a perfectly ironic moment, Adele finishes the song just as a light goes on indicating her message is being returned.

At this point, Adele had settled rather easily into the

video personification of her songs. She maintained a subtle mixture of vulnerability and hope that, in this video, never strayed from the believable.

ROLLING IN THE DEEP

In a video sense, this would be an important step. The song was already being talked about as a major player come awards season that would truly put Adele on the map. Director Sam Brown, whose list of video credits include efforts for Jay-Z, James Blunt, and Foo Fighters, knew that he would have to pick Adele's brain to come up with a vision that worked.

"The idea was really about finding different ways of expressing the anger in the words," Brown told MTV, "and then housing them in this one giant building. I was thinking about the house as her mind and the rooms as everything that was happening inside it."

The video has Adele seated in a room in a house and uses the house as a metaphor for a life in stages of renovation. Broken glass sets the tableau in motion, and then the video moves to a mysterious dancer stirring up dust and, by association, the memories that bubble up inside Adele's stoic face. The video's flaming conclusion brings full circle the concept of emotions unchained and highlights a video that is definitely more art than commerce.

SOMEONE LIKE YOU

The song was an exposed raw nerve. There was no reason to believe that the video would not be any different. But what emerged in the "Someone Like You" clip was not only a spot-on distillation of the song's somber intent but a truly classic bit of video that, in a shade under five minutes, summed up what this phase of Adele's music had been all about.

Director Jake Nava, whose long list of music video credits includes Beyoncé, Shakira, Leona Lewis, and Britney Spears, was a quick read when it came to translating the song to a video counterpart, and he looked no further than the streets of Paris for inspiration. "The location evokes romance," he told MTV. "Shooting in the early morning allows you to focus on Adele and this lonely and emotional space."

Nava knew it would be an artsy concept. He also saw it in black-and-white and with an off-kilter haze that, doubtless, brought back memories of classic Italian cinema of the '60s and '70s. Shot in Paris in the early morning hours, we see a defeated Adele walking the streets of the city as she sings her song amid a series of rotating shots of the City of Lights. Tension builds at the second chorus as she stops along the Seine River and stares out, contemplating love lost. Finally she goes to the apartment building where she sees the mystery lover who has moved on to another life with another woman. There is the heartrending moment of recollection, and maybe just a hint of longing, before the man turns and walks away, leaving Adele to have some final longing looks after him at the fade.

"Someone Like You" was something very personal and old school. And there has not been a viewer who did not have a lump in their throat . . . or a tear in their eye.

13

I CAN'T HEAR YOU

The logistics of Adele's second tour, entitled Adele Live, were a mirror image of her previous live performing schedule. Scheduled to run from March 21, 2011, to September 25, 2011, Adele Live would encompass fifty-one days: thirty-one in Europe and twenty in the all-important North American market (United States and Canada). Like the previous tour, Adele Live would stick to mid-level venues, rarely more than 3,000 seats.

There had been talks that Adele might mix in a few large festival appearances, but the artist in the singer balked, feeling that the intimacy and power of her performance would be blunted by an outdoor festival experience which often saw performers competing with a literal sea of fans. Not the perfect fit for a performer whose bread and butter was introspection and intimacy.

And as on the previous tour, Adele insisted that her stage

presence be kept fairly simple. Her band and backup singers plus some interludes that would consist of Adele's voice and a backing piano was how she wanted to present her songs. Likewise, the stage design would be a nonintrusive series of twenty-one lamp shades. The seventeen-song set list would be a mixture of songs from *21* and *19.*

Adele was now in a position to pay back the scene that spawned her and some of the individuals who helped her along the way. For the all-important North American shows, she picked the groups The Civil Wars, Plan B, and a major influence, singer Wanda Jackson. Her United Kingdom shows would showcase the talents of Amos Lee and Michael Kiwanuka.

Adele was physically and emotionally ready to hit the road. She was convinced that all the personal turmoil that had plagued the Evening with Adele tour was now far removed from her present state of mind. Adele was excited and, as those in her inner circle had most likely noticed, she was happy.

Early shows in Norway, Sweden, and Germany were considered warm-up shows in which Adele and the band could fine-tune their stage presentation.

Backup singer Henry-Davila told BBC News that she recalled that Adele was a bit tentative during those early shows. "She was a little bit more held back. She'd sing but she wouldn't move around much."

But the reports from those early shows indicated that Adele's voice and real-world attitude were already first rate. Alternately humble and joking in between songs, she was all business when she was singing, giving full vent to the power and the emotion of her songs. By the time the Adele Live tour had worked its way through Spain, Italy, Belgium, and the Netherlands, the rave reviews were piling up, praising Adele for the mastery of her live performance and the strength of her songs. It was clear that Adele had hit the ground running.

As the shows progressed, Henry-Davila could see that Adele's stage presence was definitely rounding into shape. "Towards the end of the tour she had gotten to the point where she was walking across the stage and going out into the audience."

Kiwanuka had a front row seat for the early stages of the tour and sang her praises to *The Juice*. "Seeing her sing every night and the way she carried herself was an eye-opener."

Adele's stage fright was still a constant before the shows. She would still occasionally be physically ill before the lights went down. But she always seemed to have it under control before hitting the stage, and told *Vogue*, "The worse my nerves are before a show, the better the show turns out to be."

The April 12 show in Ireland had Adele shifting into a new gear, according to those who had diligently followed the tour. It was no secret that Adele was particular psyched about the upcoming dates in the UK. She was very much in the moment of this being a homecoming and would be pulling out all the stops.

And from the moment Adele walked on stage at the O2 Academy in Leeds and said, "It's great to be back in the fucking UK," the audience was in her hands, alternately respectful and boisterous as Adele bared her soul in a live setting. It was a scene that would play out on subsequent nights in Manchester, Southampton, Birmingham, and London. Adele ended the first leg of her European tour on April 21.

Guitarist Van Der Kuil recalled that, despite her star status, she never came off as a prima donna. "When you're on the road, you don't see her much," he told *The Juice*. "But she always sticks her head into the dressing room before we go onstage and has a bit of a chat. She likes a good laugh."

Following the conclusion of the European leg of the tour, Adele literally took a week off to party. Over a five-day period she was seen out and about every night, sharing drinks and good cheer with the likes of Mark Ronson and James Corden. Adele was so wrapped up in cutting loose over the next few days that when she received a request to perform at the royal wedding of Prince William and Kate Middleton, she had to decline on the grounds of a previously booked engagement.

"I couldn't play because my barbecue had already been booked for quite some time," she told *The Sun*.

What the world would discover around this time was that a big reason Adele was most likely partying so hard was that she was coming off yet another whirlwind, very secret romance that had begun in December 2010 and had quickly flamed out. Adele dismissed this failed relationship when she told Female First that "He just doesn't love me as much as I love him." There was much speculation and no small amount of humor in the notion that this mystery fling would be the inspiration for Adele's third album, but Adele was on to more important things.

Soon she would be rediscovering America.

But not before turning twenty-three on May 5, 2011, and making an important personal decision. The all-night birthday bash saw Adele hosting a karaoke party at a local club, one in which she joined the festivities by doing a rousing rendition of the R. Kelly song "Ignition."

On the personal front, Adele decided to stop drinking. She also hinted that she was considering giving up smoking and, despite spending countless interviews defending her full-figured look, she was toying with the idea of getting a trainer and going on a weight-loss program. Adele would acknowledge her sudden turn toward a healthier lifestyle had nothing to do with the long-standing questions about her weight and anti–model figure stance. What she must have sensed was that the rigors of touring and being in the limelight required a healthier attitude, physically and emotionally.

It was midway through 2011 that Adele finally seemed to come to grips with the fact that she was not the poor little cockney girl from Tottenham anymore. In an interview with *Q*, she bemoaned the fact that she could not take public transportation anymore without being recognized. And she was finally coming to the conclusion that, like many other celebrities, she had a problem with the fact that the UK had what many would consider an overbearing tax system.

"I'm learning about taxes at the moment from my accountant," she said. "I'm mortified that I have to pay fifty percent. When I got my tax bill from (the album *19*), I was ready to go out and buy a gun and open fire."

There would be an immediate and surprisingly overwhelmingly negative backlash to her comments from people who were not stars and lived in the real world. Adele learned not to rattle the cages of working-class Brits and would acknowledge that she probably should not have opened her mouth on the subject.

How quickly Adele had risen to the top of the pop music mountain was much in evidence at that point when the singer placed No. 9 on the annual British poll of the most successful artists in the UK. The poll indicated that Adele had earned well over 6 million pounds.

During the time off before resuming Adele Live in the States, Adele continued to be the darling of the press. She was happy to talk about how the tour had gone to that point and continued to drop hints about what the future might bring.

In a conversation with *The Sun*, Adele elaborated on previous announcements that she would have a third album out by May 2012. "I have five tracks all ready to go. One of them is the INXS song 'Never Tear Us Apart' (which did not make the cut on the 21 album). One of them is a real upbeat, real girl power type of thing."

Adele Live kicked off its US/North American swing on May 12 in Washington D.C. The success of the European tour continued on stops in Philadelphia, Boston, Montreal, Toronto, and New York City. The audiences were captivated by Adele's true interpretation of classic US musical genres and her "just folks" attitude.

Adele made good on her promise to get up close and personal with fans. She was happy to pose for pictures, sign autographs, and chat with anybody who approached her on the street. And then there was the daily schedule of visits to radio stations, press interviews, and all the realities of getting the word out, which Adele was also quite happy to do.

Everything was going fine.

Until May 26.

The previous night's performance in Chicago had continued a run of first-rate performances, and pulling into Minneapolis the following day, there was no reason to think anything but perfection would be on the agenda that night at the First Avenue club.

But during the afternoon sound check, according to a report filed by the Minneapolis *StarTribune*, Adele attempted to sing, but her throat was hurting. According to the *Star-Tribune*, First Avenue general manager Nate Krantz was at the club during the sound check and observed, "She got out a few notes and then stopped. She knew that her voice was shot."

Her guitarist, Tim Van Der Kuil, remembered that day quite well. "We went in to do the sound check and she started singing and the notes just weren't there at all. It was very tough on her and she was really upset," he told *The Juice*.

Adele was taken to a local throat specialist and it was determined that the singer had come down with a severe case of laryngitis. Three hours before Adele was to perform, it was announced that throat problems had caused her to cancel the evening's performance, but that it would be rescheduled for June 22.

The doctor had strongly suggested that Adele take some time off to let her voice recover. But ever the trooper, Adele, only two days after the cancellation in Minneapolis, pronounced herself ready to do the next scheduled show in Denver on May 28.

The sound check in Denver seemed good enough for Adele to go on; however, it was obvious that the singer was struggling throughout the show and, while the audience was appreciative, Adele knew she had not given her best effort and that the laryngitis was still a lingering issue.

Still, Adele was convinced she could somehow get through, and so, against the advice of more than one member of her entourage, the tour proceeded on to Salt Lake City. Adele posted a note on her blog regarding what happened next.

"I hate to cancel, especially at such short notice. I am truly devastated. I'm here in the city (Salt Lake City) and I tried to do the sound check at the venue. But if I push through it tonight, it will take me longer to get better. Please forgive me."

Adele attempted one last shot at salvaging the tour. She hoped that by not speaking and following doctor's orders, she might be up to performing on June 4 in San Francisco. But, as reported on E! Online, any hopes for resuming the tour were dashed when her consulting specialist insisted that she take a few weeks off and have complete voice rest. Adele reluctantly agreed, and the last nine remaining dates on the current leg of the US tour were canceled. In a statement released by Adele, she said:

"I'm really frustrated. I was hoping with a week's rest I'd be better to sing again. However, there is absolutely nothing I can do but take the doctor's orders and rest some more. I'm so sorry. See you soon.

"Love, Adele."

14

THE SOUND OF SILENCE

dele flew back to London. She went into seclusion, resting her voice and contemplating what would happen next. But with little information on the state of her voice forthcoming, the tabloids picked up the story and ran with it as only they could.

The Star ran wild with the story, offering that the US tour had been canceled because a US record company executive had made a derogatory comment about Adele's weight at the start of the American leg of the tour. The tabloid also floated the theory that when Adele gets nervous on stage, her throat closes up. Most people laughed off the tabloid reports as rubbish, but Adele did not see her predicament as a laughing matter.

In an emotion-filled blog picked up by *OK* magazine and others, Adele said, "Singing is literally my life, my hobby, my love, my freedom, my job. You know how much this upsets me, how seriously I take it, and how truly devastated and annoyed I am by this."

Her concern was not helped by her doctor's speculation that Adele had not had a simple attack of laryngitis but rather a potentially more serious malady, a burst blood vessel on her vocal cords.

Adele continued to follow her doctor's orders of no singing and a strict adherence to limiting how much she spoke. Within weeks of returning to London, doctors were convinced that Adele's vocal cord issue was healing. With that news and her doctor's guarded optimism, Adele was anxious to get back and test her voice in a live setting.

That opportunity presented itself on July 7 when Adele took to the stage, for the first time since the aborted US tour, at the prestigious iTunes Festival in London. Word spread like wildfire that Adele was returning to the concert stage. And Adele was more than happy to let her legions of fans know what had transpired over the past month.

"It's basically a hole in your cord," she explained to Radio 1 DJ Chris Moyles two days before her iTunes appearance. "I sang through it and that's why it (the blood vessel) popped. "I'm better now. It's fine. I got the all clear."

The iTunes Festival was most likely thick with tension and emotion moments before Adele was scheduled to take the stage. A lot of questions would be answered, not the least of which was, could Adele once again sing at the level she had previously? . . . If at all? . . .

Over the course of a set that included "Rolling In The Deep," "Someone Like You," "Chasing Pavements," and "Turning Tables," Adele performed an emotionally charged set that had both the audience and, at one point, Adele in tears. As she walked off the stage to thunderous applause, Adele must have known in her heart and soul that she was back.

"It's like 99.9 percent better so I'm really, really happy," she told TV interviewers Dave Berry and Alexa Chung in a post-concert interview that was picked up by Oneindia. "I thought a month ago that I would never be able to sing again. So I'm really relieved. It went great and my voice isn't hurting."

Adele was brimming over with newfound excitement. She immediately went to her team and insisted that she was ready to return to America for a series of makeup shows. There were also talks of adding additional shows as a way of paying back America for the disruption of the tour. Plans were put into motion. But first there would be cautious first steps.

A truncated North American tour was pieced together for August, encompassing shows in British Columbia, Oregon, Seattle, Berkeley, Los Angeles, San Diego, Las Vegas, Salt Lake City, and St. Paul. If those shows went well and Adele's health remained strong, tentative steps were already being taken for more shows in October.

Adele was thrilled to be heading back to America and excitedly blogged, "I was having the best time on the US tour. I met some amazing people, did some fantastic shows, and played with some amazing performers. I will be happy to get back."

The best-case scenario for Adele's return to America played out on a nightly basis during those August dates. Adele sounded as good as ever, and the result was memorable shows in which there seemed a renewed power and emotion in the singer's voice. Because of the problems with the previous US visit, Adele seemed driven to get it right this time and, by the end of August, the consensus was that the bump in the road that was Adele's last visit to America had all but been forgotten.

But while her voice remained strong, a series of colds and chest infections toward the end of August were beginning to take their toll.

Adele could not believe her bad luck and expressed her growing frustrations in a *Daily Mail* story. "I can't believe it. I follow all the advice I'm given and stick to regimes, rules, and practices to the best of my ability. But it seems to not be enough."

Again, on the advice of doctors, Adele postponed a series of UK shows slated for early September as well as an appearance at the prestigious UK institution, the Mercury Prize awards ceremony. Adele would recover sufficiently by mid-September to make up the missed UK shows.

And one of those would be an appearance at the legendary Royal Albert Hall. There was some concern that Adele should continue to baby her voice, but the fact that the singer's voice had improved significantly, plus the fact that the stately Royal Albert Hall had become a must-play gig for some of the biggest names in music, ultimately dictated that she would do the show.

Adele was in fine form the night of the show, trotting out the best of her *19* and *21* albums in a powerful manner, engaging in delightful between-song patter with the audience, and to the delight and amazement of the audience, dropping a few F-bombs that seemed to echo through the prestigious venue.

The show was a rousing success and, in a purely business sense, a good move. Management and record company saw fit to do both a live CD and DVD taping of the show, with an eye toward releasing both in a timely manner to keep Adele's name and music in the public eye.

During this period, Adele finally had to come to grips with the reality that she had quickly outgrown the small clubs and halls that she had long preferred. And as the Adele Live tour entered its final dates, she would announce to audiences that her days in intimate venues were numbered.

"Too many people want to see my shows," she told a London audience, as reported by *The Guardian*. "This is the last time you will see me in a venue like this. These will be my last theater dates, as I am moving on to arenas."

But while Adele's music continued its march (with *21* having already sold 10 million albums worldwide, and the single "Rolling In the Deep" spending nine weeks at No. 1 on the Billboard charts), there were those who had taken notice of Adele's occasional physical lapses and were up front in saying that the singer might be due a prolonged hiatus from performing.

For her part, Adele was feeling like she had turned the corner on any physical ailments and was all ready to return to performing in October. But first there was a bit of personal business to deal with. A friend was getting married on October 1, and Adele had promised to serenade the happy couple. On that day, Adele got up to sing . . .

And then it happened.

15.
UNDER THE KNIFE

knew my voice was in trouble," Adele told *Vogue* of the immediate aftermath of the October wedding incident. "And obviously I cried a lot."

What had initially been diagnosed as simple laryngitis had suddenly become a lot more serious. At that point, the word that kept coming up was "hemorrhage." The word sounded harsh. The implications were even worse. Adele and her team gathered together to decide what to do next.

The first move was to cancel the remainder of Adele's touring schedule for the year. The singer confronted the announcement head-on, announcing in both blogs and management statements the reality of her situation.

"I have no choice but to recuperate properly and fully or I risk damaging my voice forever," she said. "I know it's disappointing but please have faith in me that this is only thing I can do to make sure that I can always sing and always make music for you."

Despite being up front and honest about her condition, Adele expected the tabloid press to have a field day with her condition. And so she was not surprised when stories proclaiming "Adele has cancer," "Adele is suicidal," and "Adele will never sing again" screamed out their sensationalist headlines. Adele could do nothing other than deny it was anything that dire, but until she knew for sure, sadly this malady was open season.

Adele did her best to combat the tide of gossip when she told the *Daily Mail*, "The fact is that I have never been able to fully recover from any of the problems that I have had, and then continue to rest even after I recovered, because of my touring commitments."

The upside of the announcement was that she would receive countless messages from well-wishers, including several from celebrity singers who had also had vocal-cord problems over the years. John Mayer, Elton John, Steven Tyler, Roger Daltrey, and many others suggested that Adele should consult with the stateside physician Dr. Steven Zeitels.

Dr. Zeitels, the director of the Massachusetts General Hospital Voice Center in Boston, had long been in the forefront of pioneering vocal cord procedures and had worked wonders in helping Aerosmith front man Steven Tyler and Who singer Roger Daltrey maintain their singing ability. Of particular interest to Adele was the fact that he had pioneered the use of lasers in throat surgery. Adele was heartened by Zeitels' credentials and readily agreed to fly to the States for a consultation.

Adele was encouraged by her meeting with the doctor.

"When I met him I loved him," she told *Vogue*. "He made me feel safe."

When Zeitel examined the singer he discovered a polyp on one of Adele's vocal cords. Zeitels assured the singer that fixing the problem was considered a fairly common procedure. Zeitels would not discuss the particulars of the patient's case. But the hospital, in a statement published by Reuters, stated Adele's condition was attributed to "the result of unstable blood vessels in the vocal cord that can rupture."

Many theories were floated as to why Adele's approach to singing could have caused such a problem. But Adele insisted in a conversation with *The Sun* that her problem had nothing to do with singing, but rather by her talking so much.

"I damage my vocal cords offstage, not onstage. Onstage I am fine because, apparently, I am technically great. But when I talk, I damage my voice big-time."

Adele had previously talked about giving up cigarettes, but with the possibility of her nonstop smoking habit having something to do with her voice problems, she essentially quit on the spot and vowed that she would begin to adopt a more healthy lifestyle postsurgery. There was conviction in her voice. Adele would most certainly turn her life around.

In the days leading up to the surgery, the music world was in high-gear speculation despite the medical prognosis that things would go smoothly. The rumors and gossip continued and reached such a critical mass that Adele's people were forced to issue a statement reiterating that the singer was going in for surgery to remove a polyp and that any other reports were false.

Adele's surgery was scheduled for early November 3,

2011. The surgery was routine and considered a success. Adele, in a *60 Minutes* interview, explained the procedure in layman's terms. "They put lasers down my throat, cut off the polyp, and kind of lazered the hemorrhage back together."

Adele left the hospital and returned to London. She was under orders not to speak at all for six weeks (which is nearly twice the usual recovery time), a tall order for somebody like Adele.

Paper, pencil, and the occasional chalkboard were the only way Adele could communicate during those first few weeks, and even then it was not very often because, while not in forced isolation, Adele was physically and psychologically on the mend and did not want to deal with too many people.

Adele did not say a word for three weeks. Doctor's orders.

"Not speaking was really hard," Adele would tell Anderson Cooper during her *60 Minutes* interview. "I love talking."

However, truth be known, there was really not much for the singer to do except watch as *21* continued to set the world on fire. The album had long since reached multiplatinum status worldwide. *21* had risen to phenomenal levels by the standards of the music industry. Adele's power as a performing artist could not be denied. There was some preliminary talk about the Grammys and the suggestion that Adele would do just fine come awards season.

Adele was neutral on the subject of the Grammys at that point. She agreed that winning would certainly be a high honor, but such responses were almost afterthoughts to the reality of what was going on in her life. Awards would mean nothing if she could never sing again.

Rather than sulk at her situation, Adele looked inward

and became philosophical on the notion of being silent. She looked at her vocal loss as a near-existential thing, a sign that her body was telling her to fix herself. She would never be too specific about the introspective nature of that time, but she did offer in a *Mirror* piece, "I had so much time to go over things and get over things. Now I feel really at peace."

But introspection would only carry Adele so far.

Adele soon became restless at her confinement and wanted to get out and about. But that required some way to communicate without speaking, or endless time spent writing notes. Adele figured the problem out, thanks to modern technology.

Adele had an application installed in her phone that she could type words into and the app would speak the words. In the spirit of keeping in character, Adele would also find an application that would allow her to swear.

"It is far easier to communicate using it (the app), rather than just writing everything down on paper and showing it to people," she related to *60 Minutes*.

With the freedom to actually "speak," Adele was now out and about more frequently. She would be spotted regularly at the local Starbucks or hailing a cab for a shopping trip. As ever, she was wildly approachable. One day she passed a group of builders working on the office building she was about to enter. She stopped, posed for pictures, and with her app moving a mile a minute, chatted up the workers. What she soon discovered was that news of her surgery and recovery had taken on a life of its own and she was constantly having to type out an answer to . . .

"How's your throat?" Adele related to *Vogue*. "Everybody is so worried."

The taping of Adele's Royal Albert Hall performance was now looking like a stroke of genius. With Adele on the shelf, November saw the release of the DVD *Adele Live at the Royal Albert Hall*. Rather than a stopgap measure, the DVD proved a classic example of Adele at the peak of her performing prowess: glorious moments mixed with pitch-perfect renditions of classic songs. If no new material would be forthcoming from Adele for a while, this concert would definitely keep her followers satisfied until the next phase of Adele's career kicked in.

Adele continued her slow but steady climb back to regaining her voice. By mid-December, six weeks into her postoperative recovery, Adele was given the okay to begin building up her voice. After six weeks of silence, her first step on the road back was a small one.

She was humming. In the shower, walking around her flat. On the street. For the singer, it seemed odd when her mind was telling her to burst out in song. But with her future at stake, Adele had gotten very good at following doctor's orders.

Along the path to recovery, Adele had also found an added bonus. Despite her long-held attitude of not caring about being a model body type, she suddenly found herself looking much skinnier after having lost better than twenty-five pounds. Long fond of junk food and sugary sweets, Adele had quit cold turkey when her doctors advised her that those things would hurt her stamina and impact her voice. And she had to admit that she liked the new, improved, and much slimmer Adele a lot.

The week before Christmas, Adele started to sing.

She was not belting out songs at her normal level of

emotion. In fact, she was instructed to limit her recovery song list to "Happy Birthday to You" and "The Grand Old Duke of York," songs that would properly exercise her limited vocal range at the time. And then there were the god-awful vocal exercises that Adele was forced to endure.

"Now I have to sing my songs through a straw to get my diaphragm going," she told *The Sun* of her recovery process. "I have to do all these facial movements to get my face going and it makes me look butt-ugly because my whole face vibrates. But the worst thing is that I've got this massive thing that looks like a sex toy and I've got to stick it into a bottle of water and blow."

But as she wandered through her home, took a shower, or just sang along with music, it was clear that the healing process was in the homestretch and that Adele was now sounding like Adele. Adele noticed that, with the polyp now gone, her voice was now a lot higher than it used to be.

But the most important thing was, as Adele told *Vogue*, "It still sounds like me."

As if getting her voice and, by association, her life back was not enough of a holiday present, the Grammy nominations had come through three weeks earlier. And from top to bottom, Adele was all over them.

21 received nominations for Album of the Year and Best Pop Vocal Album. "Rolling In The Deep" added nominations for Record of the Year and Song Of The Year as well as Best Short Form Video. Finally, the song "Someone Like You" received the nomination for Best Pop Solo Performance.

The normally unflappable XL President Richard Russell was happily at a near loss for words with the announcement.

He acknowledged in a Tweet My Song interview that *21* was "a very instinctive" record and that was why people liked it.

"The Grammy nominations have been the latest in a long line of slightly unreal events," he elaborated. "The whole thing has been very unorchestrated."

With the nominations, the unprecedented success of *21*, and Adele's recovery from throat surgery, the media was quick to latch on to the Cinderella story of Adele. Jonathan Dickins was often approached during this time to respond to the fairy-tale nature of the singer's success. Dickins would shrug his shoulders and admit to being at a loss to explain it.

"There was no way we could have predicted the level of success," he told *The Telegraph*. "The stars simply align. There are elements you simply have no control over."

The six nominations were extraordinary on any number of levels. The more hysterical media were proclaiming Adele as the leader of a new British Invasion. Equally newsworthy was the speculation on whether Adele would show up for the ceremonies. The last time Adele captured Grammy honors, she made it plain that she was not overwhelmed with the concept of awards but had behaved appropriately for the occasion. Spokespeople for both Adele's record label and management were quick to respond that Adele was honored by the nominations and would treat the occasion with the proper respect.

For her part, Adele had no intention of causing a scene. She acknowledged in the aftermath of the announcement that she had cried at the news and that she would love to win.

But would she be able to sing? That remained to be seen.

16.
NEW MAN

There had been rumors for some months that there was a new man in Adele's life. But those gossip items, no more than "Adele is seeing a new man," were never more than unsubstantiated quips that paled in comparison to the ongoing drama of Adele's surgery, recovery, and whether her career was suddenly over.

However, toward the latter months of 2011, it became increasingly clear that Adele was, indeed, involved. There were the occasional sightings of Adele arm in arm with a certain someone walking down the street or ducking into a club or restaurant. And by the time Adele had begun the final lap of recovering her voice, the singer was making very little attempt to hide her new boyfriend.

A *Vogue* magazine profile on Adele went into much detail and intrigue when it described how the singer interrupted a photo shoot to breathlessly run out into the street with her cell phone to make a quick call. Adele then returned, handing her cell phone to her assistant with the instructions, "He's out in the car having a smoke. If he calls, go out and bring him in."

Moments later, as presented by *Vogue*, the world got its first clear picture of Simon Konecki. Thumbnail sketch: A big, cuddly bear, bearded type. Laid-back, attentive, and not in the entertainment business. And oh yes, a much older man at age thirty-seven.

The couple met in London during summer 2011 at a meet and greet for Simon's charity organization Drop4Drop. Their politics and charitable leanings were an immediate match. That each came from completely different social strata and educational backgrounds never entered the picture. They were instantly attracted to each other, but cautious. Reportedly, from the moment they met, they had been inseparable. Things appeared to be moving fast in their relationship, so much so that during an early September concert in Glasgow, shortly before her voice problems set in, she gushed and joked quite openly with the audience about her new boyfriend.

Adele has frequently gushed in interviews about what she likes about Simon, often lapsing into little-girl giggles and longing expressions when describing her new love.

To hear the singer describe Simon, he was her dream man.

He was attentive to her needs. He was fully aware of her celebrity status but did not care or interfere in the mechanics of her career. He did not care about what other people thought of her. He was there for her in whatever capacity she required. He was proud of her and, perhaps, most important, he was a comfort to her, someone who could make Adele laugh at the drop of a hat.

"He's wonderful," Adele gushed to *Vogue*.

Simon Konecki was seemingly born on the right side of the tracks with a silver spoon in his mouth. He attended the prestigious boys school in Eton and went directly into the world of high finance, working as a director of investment for the well-known EBS Group. He traveled in high society and palled around with millionaires and upper-class socialites. But unlike the conservative circles he traveled in, Simon had a left-leaning, humanitarian soul.

In a Facebook excerpt from the organization Life Pure Water, Simon had revealed his growing disconnect with the banking world and, in particular, what he perceived as the growing divide between rich and poor, especially when it came to supplying clean water to poor, underdeveloped countries. "I felt that water was a human right and that it (dirty water) was happening. I wanted to explore why we let it happen when fixing the problem was relatively easy."

His disillusionment reached critical mass, and Simon dropped out of the banking world and founded the charity organization Drop4Drop, which is dedicated to supplying clean water to needy countries.

Simon married fashion stylist Clary Fisher in 2004. The marriage would last until 2010 and produced a daughter, now five years old.

Once Adele had turned the corner on her voice issues, her relationship with Simon left the shadows and jumped to the forefront of the tabloid pages. The most outrageous charges were that Simon was still legally married when he began dating Adele and that, even now, he was still not legally divorced. Adele had kept largely mum and never more than good-natured when discussing Simon, but these charges annoyed her to the point where she took to her own Web site to blog a response to the tabloid accusations.

"This is the first and last time I will comment on the details of my relationship with Simon. Contrary to reports in the press, Simon is divorced and has been for four years. Everyone in our lives wishes us the very best." (Simon's divorce was in 2010.)

Adele and Simon reportedly spent a blissful New Year's Eve together. And according to *US Weekly*, people were noticing a definite change in the singer since meeting Simon. The magazine reported that a source close to the couple said, "They were looking very lovey-dovey together and that Adele was smiling in a way that hasn't been seen in a long time."

The cloak of secrecy was finally lifted early in January 2012 when paparazzi snapped a series of photos of Adele and Simon on holiday in the Florida Everglades. The photos clearly showed the couple kissing passionately and embracing as only lovers do. So, for the whole world to see, Adele was now in love.

The tidal wave of speculation was building on a worldwide basis with almost daily alleged discoveries. Adele, who had long indicated she would probably be thirty before she started having children, was now reported as saying that she wanted to start having the first of as many as five or six babies within the new year. Adele and Simon were allegedly engaged and any bit of jewelry spotted on the singer's hand was immediately labeled an engagement ring. Adele and Simon were planning on adopting an Ethiopian child. Adele mania was off and running.

The only thing that was certain was that Simon would be on Adele's arm out in public for the first time at the 2012 Grammy Awards.

What was less certain was whether Adele would sing.

17

IN THE DEEP END

The Grammy Awards were a mere six weeks away. Adele was champing at the bit to make her singing comeback at the ceremonies, which would be televised worldwide. But she was not sure if she could do it.

One person who was pretty sure she could was Dr. Steven Zeitels. The doctor who operated on Adele and who had examined her several times during the intervening months told the *Los Angeles Times* that she was definitely on schedule.

"When I do that kind of operation, the typical time someone starts singing again is three and a half to five weeks (after surgery)."

Not everybody else in Adele's camp was quite as certain. Her manager, Jonathan Dickins, offered in a Perez Hilton column that "Adele was obviously nervous" and that she was "showing great character by considering going into the deep end by making her comeback in front of the largest audience in the world."

Worst-case scenarios were most likely as prevalent in Adele's thoughts as were the possibilities of a comeback of classic proportions. Adele was probably feeling the pressure of coming back at full strength and knew that half stepping her vocals just would not do. But, she must have felt, what would happen if she went for her trademark powerful voice and came up short? Sleepless nights were probably in order for the singer in the days leading up to a final decision whether or not to make a very public comeback and sing at the Grammys.

After much thought, Adele contacted the Grammy producers and said that yes, she would sing. And she would be quick in letting her legions of fans know that she was, indeed, back.

"I'm a being singing at the Grammys," she said in a blog. "It's been so long that I started to forget that I was a singer."

Her songwriting partner, Dan Wilson, told *PopMatters* he was confident in Adele's decision to sing at the Grammy show. "Adele does not put herself in dumb situations. She's got really impeccable judgment when it comes to her artistry."

Adele had much to distract her in her postsurgery months. Her love life for one thing. The recovery process which, in interviews, she often played for laughs. But as the Grammys grew ever closer, she began to take the prospect of singing and then touring seriously. The singer was definitely concerned about very long tours and had remarked at one point in the healing process that two-hundred-date tours would definitely be out of the question in the foreseeable future and most likely forever.

There had been hints of a mid-May 2012 return to the studio but, to everyone's knowledge, Adele had not been actively writing and, even if she had, who knew if she could sing any new songs?

Into late January, Adele knew it was finally time to test the waters. And that opportunity arose with a request by the venerable television talk show *60 Minutes* to do a major piece that would encompass a tour of her grounds and estate in Sussex, questions outlining her recovery from the surgery, and some rather easy softball questions about celebrity and such. But the clincher was that, for the first time since her surgery, the piece would end with Adele singing "Rolling In The Deep."

Adele's handlers were excited and nervous. If she could pull it off on *60 Minutes*, there would be no question that she could sing at the Grammys. Adele was convinced that her voice was back and that she could do an intimate concert-for-one with interviewer Anderson Cooper and the millions who would, doubtless, be tuning in.

True to the prediction of a monster audience, millions tuned in for the airing of Adele's *60 Minutes* segment, which aired less than a week before the February 12 awards show. Everybody with even a passing interest in the singer was holding their breath. Adele's had been a fairy-tale story to this point.

It would be nice to have a happy ending.

Anderson Cooper was a polished interviewer with a knack

for putting even the most reluctant subject at ease. And in the early elements of the piece, Adele seemed relaxed.

As the segment neared its end, Cooper almost matter-of-factly suggested that Adele might sing something. Adele sang for the first time in five months. Her voice, presented in simple a cappella fashion, was as haunting and emotional as it had ever been. She hit all the right notes and was not out of tune. The sheer joy on her face was unmistakable. Adele's return to center stage found the singer singing as well, if not better, than she had before the polyp was found. Adele heaved a sigh of relief.

Her world was back where it should be.

Adele knew things would be different as Simon and she winged across the waters to Los Angeles for the 2012 Grammy Awards ceremony. The last time Adele took home top Grammy honors, in 2009, she was the new kid on the block, totally mesmerized by the glitz, glamour, and the literal wave of musical icons she had brushed shoulders with and was much in awe of.

Three years later, the only difference was that she was now a peer among the great musicians and performers of the day, and one that the oddsmakers felt would walk off with all the top prizes of the evening.

The Grammys would also be the big coming-out party for the couple. As they went from airport to limo to hotel and finally to the red carpet, Adele and Simon were arm in arm and displaying their affections for the paparazzi and the world to see. Adele was truly happy and was now glad to share her joy with the world.

Sadly, the celebratory nature of The Grammys would be

dashed twenty-four hours earlier with the sudden, unexpected death of legendary singer Whitney Houston. Houston's death cast a cloud over the proceedings as arrivals for the pre-Grammy parties and those on their way down the red carpet were bombarded with questions about Houston. The show's producers would spend a chaotic night trying to fine-tune the evening's proceedings to include recognition of the singer's life and their sadness at her passing.

Adele's guitarist, Tim van der Kuil, recalled in a feature in *The Juice* what it was like when Adele and the band came in for the sound check mere hours before the ceremonies were set to begin.

"It was amazing," he said. "There was Paul McCartney rehearsing the last four songs from *Abbey Road*. We looked around the auditorium's seating plan and we saw the names Bruce Springsteen, Dave Grohl, and Alicia Keyes."

Inside the theater, waiting for the show to begin, Adele was once again a bundle of nerves as she sat with her man. Adele had been scheduled to sing early in the show and she had to wonder how her emotional rendition of "Rolling In The Deep" would resonate with the now largely somber proceedings.

She would not have long to wait. Shortly after an emotional opening monologue by the evening's host, L.L. Cool J, and a few awards, Adele walked out on stage to thunderous applause. Adele looked at the audience, smiled, and started to sing.

Her sound man, Zavaglia, remembered the moment with *We Out Here*. "She was very nervous going into this. She ended up nailing it. You can even see it. As soon as she got through the first chorus she was confident and really enjoying herself."

Adele's vocals were nearly spiritual as she rolled easily into the now-familiar tale of the obstacles one faces when love dies. Adele delved within for the emotion, the pain, the hope, and the strength to move on that the lyrics spoke of. You could see it in Adele's eyes. She had reached down deep for her first time back in the spotlight. The standing ovation and the thunderous applause from some of the biggest names in the music industry that greeted the conclusion of "Rolling In The Deep" was real.

As were the tears.

Zavaglia recalled what happened next. "Ordinarily she would have been whisked back to her dressing room to change and then brought back to her seat. But she waited backstage for us so she could hug every member of the band and crew and say thank you. It was really beautiful. I got a little choked up."

It would be Adele's night, a night that grew more gratifying as Adele returned again and again to the stage to accept all six of her Grammys. Adele could not hold back her enthusiasm as she finally stepped up to accept the Grammy for Best Album Of The Year—she thanked the one person who had been there from the beginning. "First of all I want to say, 'Mum . . . girl done good.'

"This record is inspired by something that is really normal, and everyone's been through it . . . a rubbish relationship," she continued in her acceptance speech. "It's gone on to do things that . . . I can't tell you how I feel about it. It has been the most life-changing year."

The inevitable post-Grammy press conference question was what was next. Adele excitedly told reporters that she was "Going to take some time off to be happy and then to write a happy record."

As if to punctuate the point, the singer and her beau, after appearances at post-Grammy parties, took off for Big Sur for what the anxious press was describing as "some private time."

In the hours and days that followed her Grammy triumph, Adele was a rush of emotions as she dealt with the press and the seemingly never-ending adulation. There was the infamous quote, said in the emotion of her Grammy wins, that she was going to take "four or five years off" because if she was constantly working her relationships inevitably failed. Her record company and management must have inwardly winced at the prospect of no new product. They would acknowledge that they would give Adele all the time she needed to get back to recording and touring. But there was an audible sigh of relief when Adele quickly backtracked on the statement and indicated any break from the business would not last that long.

"Four or five years?" she joked. "It's more like four or five days."

"I'm in it for the long run," she said in a Postnoon feature. "I don't want to be disposable. I'm not scared of losing this. I won't come out with new music until it is better than *21*.

"I don't want to release any shit."

For now Adele was young, successful beyond words, and head over heels in love, and she was going to experience it all on her terms.

How powerful a force Adele had become was evident in the week following the Grammys when a bounce in the sales of *21* resulted in 730,000 copies sold in that seven-day span.

Adele's run-around awards season would make one final lap two weeks after the Grammys, and it was an honor that Adele was particularly keen on. The 2012 BRIT Awards had nominated the singer for honors for Best British Female Solo Artist and British Album of the Year. Adele must have felt her hometown attitudes in these nominations and was nearly as excited at her prospects as she had been for her Grammy awards.

Then tragedy struck.

Mere days before the ceremony, Adele's grandmother Rose had a heart attack. Adele was distraught at the news and raced to the hospital to be at her grandmother's side. At one point, she was ready to cancel her BRIT Awards appearance. But when her grandmother's prognosis for recovery improved, she carried on.

The February 21 televised live BRIT Awards went well, with Adele winning the Best British Female Artist award. But as live events often do, the BRIT Awards were running long by the time Adele returned to the stage to accept the evening's coveted British Album Of The Year. As she began her acceptance speech, the show's host, comedian James Corden, stepped in and indelicately waved Adele off so that the band Blur could perform the show's closing song.

Adele was incensed. In a spontaneous show of defiance, she raised her middle finger in the classic "up yours" salute and walked indignantly off the stage. The incident instantly became the "news" of the event and Adele would later be mobbed by reporters.

"I got cut off during my speech and flung the middle finger. But that finger was to the 'suits' of the BRIT Awards, not to my fans."

There were immediate and heartfelt apologies from the producers of the show. But the one thing that would be most remembered was that Adele had made her point . . .

As only Adele could.

18.
HAUNTED

ith the success of Grammy and BRIT Awards triumphs behind her and love fully in bloom, Adele began addressing the issue of a new place to call home. An admitted city girl with deep London roots, Adele had long been convinced that she would never leave the hustle and bustle of London. But she had come to realize, in the aftermath of her surgery scare, that the pollution inherent in the big city could have long-term consequences for her health and, particularly, her voice.

There was also the strong desire to live closer to Simon, who lived in nearby Brighton Beach.

Truth be known, Adele was probably also looking to exercise her considerable wealth and was looking for a purchase of a home as a sign that she had really arrived as a celebrity.

Adele was being particular in what she wanted to purchase, but she soon found the perfect transition home, a twenty-five-acre estate in West Sussex that once served as a convent. What Adele found was that any sense of a religious structure had long since been replaced by a tennis court, a helicopter pad, two swimming pools, a media center, and a ten-room mansion. It went without saying that Simon would be a regular visitor at the mammoth estate. Adele was keen on the history of the estate and the many acres of land and felt she could do worse in a rental for a transitional home.

Adele paid $24,000 a month in rent on the property, which was valued at $11 million.

Adele felt she was in paradise as she wandered the halls and inspected more rooms under one roof than she had ever seen. But paradise would only last a few days.

Alone in the sprawling mansion, Adele soon began to hear things that, she told *The Sun*, "made her jump." In her rush to escape the city, the singer had not considered the possibility that her new home might be haunted. But when she began hearing the noises in the night, her imagination and fear took over her thinking. She insisted that she could not spend another night in the house alone and hired a former chauffeur-turned-bodyguard to move into the house with her and to be at her side wherever she went.

As if the possible ghosts were not enough, Adele found out soon after moving in that a public walkway literally ran right past her front door. Adele had gotten used to the reality of being a celebrity and the fact that paparazzi would literally be camped at her front door when she lived in the city. But now, with a sudden increase in concern about her safety, Adele went out and hired a full-time security staff to patrol her sprawling estate and be a constant presence at her home.

Her dream house was suddenly turning into a much larger expense and headache than she had bargained for.

In what appeared to be a half-serious attempt at dealing with the ghost issue, Adele rang up her friend, singer Robbie Williams, who was an avid follower of all things paranormal, and suggested that Williams and his wife come down for a ghost-hunting expedition on the grounds. The offer garnered a lot of press, but Williams never took her up on it.

The added security measures did not help Adele's fragile state of mind, and it was only a matter of weeks before she was once again looking for another home.

Before she had settled on her rental, Adele had spent some months looking into buying a house in the beachside community of Brighton. As this was where Simon lived, such a move seemed to make perfect sense. But Brighton was pricey and Adele, initially, did not feel comfortable with the hefty price tag a purchase like that would bring. But this time around, money was seemingly no object as she laid out a reported $5 million for a house with what had been described as a "gorgeous" view of the ocean. A house that did not contain ghosts.

Adele was so excited by the purchase that she began telling anyone who would listen about her grand plans for the house. She was going to plant a vegetable garden, lay down a concrete walkway, and along the way . . .

"Get married and have some kids," she told the *Mirror*.

Much was made of the purchase and the fact that Adele

and Simon would now be together in the lap of luxury and relationship bliss. But what the purchase ultimately represented went much deeper than that for Adele.

For the young girl who grew up in modest flats and with limited means, the house represented the fact that she had overcome the odds and, through her talent, had arrived at the pinnacle of success.

For Adele, the welcome mat was truly out.

19.
UP TO THE MINUTE

The big news entering 2012? It should have been Adele's live rendition of "Make You Feel My Love" (recorded at a much earlier radio session at WXPN) that would be appearing on the charity tribute album *Chimes Of Freedom: The Songs Of Bob Dylan, Honouring 50 Years Of Amnesty International.* But the most earthshaking bit of Adele business into the new year was . . .

Adele and Simon had gone on a diet.

Beginning with the new year, the couple announced that they had gone on an all-vegetarian diet. According to reports, the diet, coupled with an aggressive exercise routine that included jogging and Pilates, was working and, by April, the dieters were seen out and about, a literal shadow of their former selves. Headlines across the world blared out that Adele had lost fourteen pounds.

Less than a month later, *People* magazine jumped on the

Adele weight-watch bandwagon when they trumpeted a twenty-five-pound weight loss for the singer and the breathless report that Adele was spotted eating tofu in a Brighton restaurant.

Adele's comedian friend Alan Carr was more than happy to burst the media's speculative balloon. The real reason for Adele's weight loss, he told *Heat,* was . . . "The only reason she's lost all that weight is because she's stopped drinking. She had Chicken McNuggets at my place the other night. She's the least showbizzy person I know."

Adele was probably having a good laugh that her weight loss had become breaking news in the world of celebrity journalism. Adele had gotten so famous that anything she did, no matter how trivial, was cause for a banner headline.

Ironically, it was during a February 6 guest editorship at *Metro World News* magazine in Paris that prominent and somewhat offbeat fashion designer Karl Lagerfeld chose to set off a firestorm centered around the question of Adele and weight.

"The thing at the moment is Adele. She is a little too fat," he was quoted as saying. "But she has a beautiful face and a divine voice."

The response to Lagerfeld's remark was quick and resoundingly negative, with stars like Madonna coming to Adele's defense, as well as everyday people flooding the Internet with angry anti-Lagerfeld attacks. Adele's immediate response was to take the high road. "I never wanted to look like models on the covers of magazines," she told *People.* "I represent the majority of women and I'm very proud of that."

Lagerfeld backtracked on his comment, claiming that what he said had been taken out of context. He apologized to the singer and offered a collection of pricy Chanel handbags as a make-up gift. End of story.

To the world at large, Adele seemed to be doing nothing more than having a much-needed rest. Success and stress had both been constants in the previous years. Nobody would blame the singer if she took all of 2012 off. But the reality was that her fans hoped she would not.

The reality was that much of what Adele was doing in her off time was very un-celebrity-like. In fact longtime friend comedian Alan Carr told *The Sun* that Adele had become pretty much a homebody of late.

"She's always around my house or I'm around her house," he said. "We open up a pack of HobNobs (a snack food), have a cup of tea, and watch *Four in a Bed* (a reality show). She doesn't drink or smoke. It's like being around a nun."

Although Adele's family was reportedly thrilled that the singer was in a loving relationship, public comment had been almost nonexistent. Adele's mother had continued to be notoriously press shy, as had her immediate family. Consequently, there was the breathless tabloid speculation that Adele's family was not thrilled with her new man.

But the no comment drought was broken early in the year when Adele's grandmother Doreen Adkins gave a snippet to *The Sun*. "I'm over the moon that she's found love. So is my daughter, Adele's mum. The whole family is happy for her."

In the wake of Adele's Grammy sweep and the outstanding results in the BRIT Awards, it was not surprising that *21* continued a rapid sales rate and that UK sales records and famous names crumbled in the album's wake. Between February and March 2012, Adele's album leapfrogged over Michael Jackson's *Bad*, Pink Floyd's *Dark Side of the Moon*, and Dire Straits' *Brothers in Arms* on the all-time British sales charts.

Even as Adele continued to take a breather, other channels of opportunity began to open up. It was announced that the singer's music, and quite possibly the singer herself, would be part of a massive closing ceremony, honoring British creativity, at the 2012 UK Summer Olympics. And word was that Adele and the progressive rock group Muse were neck and neck in an informal poll, that was reportedly being monitored by studio executives, as to who would write and perform the title track to the upcoming James Bond movie *Skyfall*.

No less a personage than Tom Jones, who sang the title track on the early Bond film, *Thunderball*, thought that Adele would be the perfect choice for a Bond song and that she would carry on in the noble tradition of other British Bond film singers, such as Shirley Bassey. As always, there were people lining up on either side of the Bond song derby. Diehard fans who felt Adele could do no wrong were thrilled at the news. Non-Adele followers of a more progressive bent were all for Muse. Who would land the coveted gig remained to be seen.

Adele was confident enough in her chances at the Bond song that she revealed in a *Sun* feature that producer Paul Epworth and she had been working on an appropriate James Bond theme song since October of 2011. She had reportedly already written the lyrics before her throat problems surfaced and, into the new year, Epworth and Adele had stolen away on occasion to work on the music. Adele would continue to remain tight-lipped about any specifics of the project, which only added to the mystery and the suspense. Adding further intrigue was the fact that nobody at the film studio level would make it official.

A long list of top music stars that included Paul McCartney, Alicia Keyes, and Carly Simon had used the Bond theme music assignment as a sign that they had crossed over from mere stardom to something much bigger through the gate that was James Bond. However, in recent years, those theme songs did not, for the most part, translate into hit singles for the artists themselves. The consensus was that an Adele song would easily end that drought and cross over into the rarified air of a movie sound track commercial hit.

But as far as any new material beyond the Bond song, she would only hint that her writing process, as in the past, was being driven by her emotions. Which, given her current relationship status, must have been at a fairly high level.

"I imagine I'll be twenty-five or twenty-six by the time my next record comes out," she told *Billboard*. "There will be no new music until it's good enough and I'm ready."

Since *21* and the advent of Adele as a music superstar, many top artists have hinted that they would like to hitch their wagon to the singer's current star power. Late in 2011, Jay-Z and Adele had a low-key but apparently quite productive business lunch during which the possibility of collaborating musically was discussed, as was the possibility that Jay-Z's wife and longtime Adele fan, Beyoncé, was interested in collaborating with the singer. Adele seemed keen to work with Beyoncé, often citing her admiration for the artist and her career as well as the fact that she had been listening to the singer since she was eleven years old. Observers of the music scene termed such a pairing a match made in heaven and said that such a collaboration was inevitable and that the results would be of equal prominence to any Adele song.

Another name on the singer's collaboration wish list was the group Mumford & Sons and, in particular, lead singer Marcus Mumford.

"His voice goes right through me," she told *New Musical Express*. "His voice reminds me of the first time I heard Etta James and how that made me feel."

Much was also made of the recent overtures by both Cher and Lady Gaga to collaborate with Adele and, according to the Web site Celebitchy, Cher became more than a little miffed when Adele would not return her e-mails.

Word out of the just-concluded BRIT Awards was that George Michael and Adele had also gotten quite friendly and that a collaboration between the pair was being talked up.

The most recent attempt at hitching one's wagon to Adele's star was Usher who, in a rather self-serving and surprisingly candid comment to Capital FM, indicated that he "loved Adele" and thought that "the world needs an Usher and Adele record." At one point Madonna told the press that she would like to collaborate with Adele and revealed that she was trying to get Adele to perform with her as part of the recent Super Bowl halftime show until the singer developed her throat problems.

Adele was the hot star of the moment, and so these overtures did not come as a surprise. The reality was that a number of those artists who had approached Adele were sorely in need of a hit record or their careers were, at least temporarily, in decline. Consequently, it was easy to read "ulterior motive" into many of the suggested team-ups.

Adele was flattered that so many people she admired wanted to work with her but did not seem in any great hurry to do a side project, adding further speculation that the singer was already secretly at work on her follow-up to *21*.

Adele's unchallenged perch at the top of the Billboard charts finally came to an end in March when Bruce Springsteen's album *Wrecking Ball* took the No. 1 spot, knocking *21* down to No. 2. But this admittedly microscopic step back was more than balanced out when it was announced that Adele had passed David Bowie on the all-time UK sales list and was rapidly closing in on Prince.

When she was not discussing her love life, the inevitable next question was when the next album was coming. While not too specific on when, she did hint around that her next album might well be an all-acoustic country album that she would produce.

Adele was talking country music with the fervor of the newly converted and indicated she might have to relocate to the US Midwest and South for a time in order to soak up the vibe and the history that had spawned the genre.

In the meantime, there seemed to be a lot of life left in the run of *21*. By March, the third single off the album, "Set Fire To The Rain," had made its way to No. 1 on the Billboard charts. And a fourth single, "Rumor Has It," was already in the pipeline and ready for release.

Four singles off a hit album is not uncommon. But the naysayers in the critical world were now beginning to grumble at the notion of possibly five or more singles and the lack of new material on the horizon. Although nobody at Adele's label was saying so publically, it was a safe bet that an already healthy bottom line would certainly be helped by new Adele songs.

But XL was not without additional stopgap measures if Adele was slow in coming around. A greatest hits album, although a bit on the crass side, could be cobbled together from the first two albums. So could any number of live performances. And if they dug deep enough, there had to be outtakes, alternative versions, and an unused original song or cover to satisfy fans. Ideally, this was not the best way to handle things but, when you had an artist who conducted business on her own terms, it always helped to have a Plan B.

News of yet another single off *21* reignited the call for Adele to truly test her voice with some semblance of a tour in 2012. Offers had been coming in on an almost daily basis from promoters looking to cash in on Adele's recovery and the fact that she had not completed either of her previous world tours without difficulties. Millions of dollars were allegedly on the table for everything from a one-off festival appearance to a multidate European tour. There was also talk of a very short US tour. When Adele responded that she was not ready to truly test her voice with a tour, promoters began to grumble.

There were questions anew about whether Adele had recovered sufficiently from her throat surgery to attempt even a moderate-length tour. There were rumors that while Adele was physically up to the rigors of performing, mentally she was not ready.

In response, Adele's manager, Jonathan Dickins would be cautiously optimistic in a March interview with *Rolling Stone*.

"Adele loved the touring she's done in the past," he declared. "At the same time, we want to make sure that we can get through it properly. We still have to be mindful of nursing that voice back to full fitness."

Dickins reemphasized the fact that they were not thinking short-term when it came to Adele's career when he talked to *Billboard* after a night of post-Grammy celebration. "Like any injury, you have to build your strength back up. I'm not going to drive her mad."

Adele acknowledged a desire to tour again but did not see anything but the occasional one-off show happening in the coming year. She also took every opportunity to reiterate her anti-festival stance (which, given her presurgery statements to the contrary, was considered a possible change of heart) and that she would probably never embark on a super-lengthy concert tour again.

Accordingly, the question of touring was put on the back burner by management and the label, the better to leave Adele in a relaxed state that would eventually produce a new album.

Adele's long-standing anti-branding attitude was constantly under assault with offers for commercial endorsements for both serious and ridiculous products a constant temptation. One of the more outrageous, but apparently serious offers, was $1.6 million for Adele to do commercials for a new dating Web site called The Big and The Beautiful. Adele laughingly turned the offer down and, with the prospect of millions of dollars for Adele to lend her image or music to commercials, the singer remained true to her art.

"I think it's shameful when you sell out," she said in no uncertain terms in a *G Magazine* interview. "I don't want my name anywhere near another brand. I don't want to be tainted and I don't want to be in everybody's face."

She also stood by her anti-talent-show stance when the idea was floated that Adele might take a very lucrative offer to become a judge on *The X Factor*. It had not been the first time Adele had encountered TV talent show rumors. She did in fact relent, and sang on the results show episode in May 2011 of *Dancing with the Stars* and reportedly had a good bit of fun with the experience. At one point, she was reportedly being courted to make an appearance on *American Idol*. And her feathers were definitely ruffled when the musical director of *The Voice* indicated that Adele would not make the cut on the aforementioned *X Factor* because of her looks. Given her current stature in the music industry, Adele was perfectly justified in being annoyed at the insult. Adele's answer to talent show requests of any kind at that point was an emphatic no.

The not surprising aspect of Adele's rise to prominence was that people were rushing to cash in on her popularity in amusing ways. One enterprising producer had quickly cobbled together an Adele live tribute show featuring an Adele impersonator. A totally unauthorized documentary on the singer was rushed out. Adele's management was keeping an eye on such things and was diligent in addressing anything that appeared to cast a negative light on the singer.

An amusing sidelight to the mania for all things Adele was reported by the *Lancashire Telegraph*. Lareena Mitchell, who had been performing an Adele tribute show for the past three years, and who reportedly looked and sounded a lot like the singer, had stepped into the breech when rapper Tinie Timpah had failed to get Adele to perform some vocals on his latest single "Come Back Around." Mitchell would later go on to headline a festival of pop star tribute singers.

With so little hard news to report through March 2012, it seemed inevitable that a new round of rumor and gossip would make Adele headlines. It would be the *Sunday Mirror* reporting that the man who inspired the songs on *21* and who had long remained a mystery was a part-time DJ named Ned Biggs. While Biggs was not forthcoming, his mother had a clear recollection of Adele and her son dating and occasionally going camping. Adele's management responded with the expected denial that Biggs was the mystery inspiration behind *21* but would not say that Adele and Biggs had never dated.

In a matter of days another alleged ex-boyfriend was dragged into the light when *Heat* magazine proclaimed that former photographer Alex Sturrock was actually the mystery boyfriend and the inspiration behind *21*. The reality of this report was partially fueled by a series of photographs on Sturrock's Web site—informal, fun poses as well as some art shots—that indicated that Sturrock did know the singer. Again, no word from Adele or her people to confirm or deny. Consequently, this latest attempt to unmask the love bandit behind *21* would carry more weight.

The identity of the mystery boyfriend was taking on a ridiculous life of its own, with the gossip mills working overtime in getting untold mileage out of speculation on who the inspiration for Adele's music had been. And who he was pushed some mighty angry buttons in hard-core Adele fans. Sturrock was probably wise to lay low on the matter. But with Adele now in a very public relationship, it was also safe to say that the story was losing steam. At the end of the day, the good news was that even those who lived and died by tabloid headlines just did not care who the mystery lover was.

Adele's shoot-from-the-hip attitude was well known and it surfaced again in April. Still fuming from what she considered the lack of respect shown by the BRIT Awards organizers, Adele let it be known that she was considering returning her awards. On the surface, the slight would appear to have been minor. But Adele took it seriously and, typical Adele, she was taking no prisoners.

After a couple of months of a seemingly flat news cycles surrounding the singer, Adele once again captured the headlines during an interview with the French radio station NRJ, in which her recording plans were once again front and center.

"There will be a new song, probably coming out near the end of the year," she said, adding fuel to the rumor that she had already landed the song for the new James Bond movie. "But that depends on how quickly I can write new songs."

What Adele collaborator Dan Wilson was finding out was that there were plenty of fans who were willing to help the singer out. Wilson had been literally deluged with song ideas from naïve fans hoping that Wilson would forward their CDs and MP3s to Adele. Wilson sent out polite form rejection letters and links to blogs explaining the reality of the music industry.

In response to when a new Adele album might be forthcoming, she told NRJ, "It probably won't be for a good two years. I have to write another record. If I didn't write my own songs, I'd be out next week with a new album. But, because I write my own songs, I have to take some time and live a bit. I don't think I'll feel the pressure for the next album to be as big as the last one because I know that's not really possible."

Former BRIT classmate and pop star Jessie J had addressed this very issue shortly after the Grammys when she told *The Telegraph* that Adele should not rush any new music. "Realistically, Adele has set the bar so high that, even if she came back in two or three years time, I'm sure the bar will still be there. She could bring out music she wants, when she wants, and people will still appreciate it."

Jessie J was most likely spot-on in her thinking that, at this point, Adele could do no wrong. It was almost a certainty that a third album would run the critical gauntlet of comparison with *21*. But it was also equally certain that a third Adele album would also be platinum on the day of release. Given those parameters, a lesser artist might be tempted to just release anything. Adele was most certainly not a lesser artist.

The hinted report of new music took off like a shot with new round of speculation that new Adele music would soon be in the offing. But was the announcement for real or was Adele just playing games with the media?

There was some media speculation that, because Adele was now in a loving relationship, she was not in the right frame of mind to write the kind of songs that had made her famous. On the other side, there were those predicting a new musical direction for the singer, one inspired by happiness.

The juggernaut that was *21* had continued into the new

year, and on April 5 the album was deemed the biggest-selling album of 2012 so far. The success Adele was having on such a massive level inevitably brought speculation about how long it would last—before the mania and reality of the Adele movement would come crashing down. Some speculated that her insistence on doing new music when she was ready would be a turn off to the notoriously fickle pop audience, who had a history of turning to new heroes after a point if their current idols didn't keep releasing music. Others pointed out that the insane level of media saturation would eventually begin to annoy musical purists.

But nobody could argue Adele's current success and the biggest compliment was in the fact that, behind the scenes, A&R people from both major and independent labels all over the world were beating the bushes for an "Adele type," somebody who could do Adele-type songs, sing like Adele, and grab onto some semblance of the current interest in angst-ridden young female singer-songwriters. By association, anyone who had anything to do with the production of either of Adele's albums was being hounded by singers and managers looking for the Adele magic.

"A lot of American singers are reaching out to me," producer Paul Epworth told *The Salt Lake Tribune*. "But the problem is that they are asking for something that sounds like Adele. What they would end up getting is something that sounds electronic."

The search for the new Adele sounded tacky and exploitive and, to a large degree, it was just that. But this sincerest form of flattery has been played out since there has been popular music.

And with Adele's current timetable for new music uncertain, who was to say that another "Adele type" could not
fill in?

But for now, Adele stood alone, a force of nature that
could not be stopped.

Also making big Adele news on that day were tabloid
reports that the love of Adele's life was planning on popping
the question on May 5, the singer's twenty-fourth birthday.
These reports pointed to the fact that Adele had been sport-
ing a rather large ring in recent months that, perhaps, indicated that the happy couple were already engaged. Typical of
the gossip press, it was all vague and insubstantial but, like
all good gossip, it was tantalizing.

Adele's idyllic state of mind as a new homeowner received
a jolt in early April when she discovered her private, ocean-
front home was being threatened by a neighbor who, unbeknownst to Adele, had filed for and received a property
extension permit that would allow him to add a pool and
decking to his property that would overlook Adele's home.
Adele was not thrilled. The result of this intrusion would be
handled in the courts. Decision pending.

The growing impact of British performers and, in particular, Adele was made all the more prominent in early April
when Adele came in No. 1 on an international poll of the
most popular performers in pop music. Of equal impact was
that the top five of the list contained four women. As an
afterthought, it would soon be announced that Adele's *21*
captured International Album Of The Year at Canada's prestigious Juno Awards.

Back in the UK, Adele was having such a positive, uplifting impact on the financially struggling British population that no less a light than former Prime Minister Gordon Brown sent the singer a personal letter of gratitude that read "With the troubles the country is in financially, you are a light at the end of the tunnel."

On a more international level, the economic side of the music press chimed in with the news that the massive sales of the album *21* during 2011 was considered a major factor in the slight rebound in record sales from the previous year and had, at least temporarily, slowed what many were considering the inevitable demise of the industry.

With those accolades came the inevitable financial ramifications of Adele's impact. On April 10 it was announced that Adele was No. 1 on the vaunted list of the UK's richest young performers. The report indicated that Adele was worth a reported 20 million pounds and that 14 million of that had been earned in the past year alone. It was little wonder that Adele felt she could take her time in deciding her next move. Truth be known, Adele never had to work another day in her life if she so desired. But it went without saying that she would not rest on her laurels.

Adele's next big move would actually be the continued upgrading of her Brighton Beach home. Adele had long hinted at an in-home studio, and she finally pulled the trigger when it was announced that the singer had laid out a reported $2 million pounds for that project and an eco-friendly update of solar panels. Many speculated that Simon was the one who had indoctrinated Adele into the importance of helping the environment.

In a move that may easily qualify Adele for sainthood,

news broke in mid-April that Adele, with the support of XL Recordings, had awarded workers within the company a one-thousand-pound bonus for their contributions in helping the album *21* achieve multiplatinum status.

The album *21* continued to have more lives than the proverbial cat. After being bumped from the top of the charts by Bruce Springsteen and then Madonna, the album suddenly leaped back into the No. 1 slot, supplanting Madonna's surprisingly short stay at No. 1. For many observers, it was the literal passing of the torch from one generation of superstar to the next.

The at-large impression that Adele was laying low with her new love and/or working in secret was temporarily replaced by a real-life Adele sighting in mid-April. Reportedly, Adele was spotted with friends by the astonished waitstaff in a South Wales diner. What made this trifling report a bit more interesting was the rumor that the singer was in the area to put in an unannounced live performance at the nearby Laugharne Weekend Music Festival. A bemused organizer of the event said it was news to him but that if Adele did show up, he was sure they could find a performing slot for her.

Adele and her beau returned to the singer's roots when they were spotted among the cheering throng at Wembley Stadium for a soccer contest featuring the Tottenham Hotspurs. Adele's beloved Hotspurs lost the game 5–1, but the singer appeared to have had a great time indulging her passion for her hometown team.

This had not been the first time that Adele and Simon had been out and about and very public in the last few months. Reporters on the London tabloid beat had captured the couple eating at several restaurants in London and, on one occasion, shopping for vintage items in West London shops. In another sighting, Adele was seen walking around London shops, her hair messed and looking like she had literally just stepped out of the shower. Long story short, all these sightings indicated that the couple, together and singularly, looked very happy.

Which lent credence to Adele's recent proclamations that now that she was in love, she was finished with the sadness that permeated her first two albums, and that the long-anticipated third album would be very positive in tone. Informal opinion along the blogosphere was equally divided: some were looking forward to the change in tone, while others mourned the possible loss of melancholy.

Adele's long-established hold on the US charts reached yet another milestone in mid-April when *21* spent its twenty-fifth week atop the Billboard charts, effectively eclipsing the previous record holder, Prince and the Revolution's *Purple Rain* sound track album, which had held the coveted spot in 1984 and '85. The long-charted *21* was continuing to sell at a phenomenal pace, averaging an estimated 150,000 copies a week in the United States.

The honor that Adele was particularly keen about came April 17, when it was announced that she had received four nominations for the prestigious UK Ivor Novello songwriting awards. As always, Adele was humbled by any honors that focused on her creative efforts. These nominations were particularly gratifying because she would be up against two contemporaries she deeply admired, Kate Bush and PJ

Harvey. *21* received a nomination for Best Album while "Rolling In The Deep" and "Someone Like You" shared the nod for Best Song and Most Performed Work.

The continuing mystery of whether Adele would truly do the next Bond film title track picked up a bit more steam when a reporter for *HitFix* asked the film's producer, Barbara Broccoli, about the Adele rumor. She said, "Nobody has been confirmed yet but it would be great if she would do it."

Well into April, Adele continued to rack up honors. The prestigious Billboard Awards announced that the singer had received a total of eighteen nominations for ceremonies that would take place late in May. These included Top Artist, Top Female Artist, Top Billboard 200 Artist, Top Pop Album (*19*), and Top Hot 100 Song for "Rolling In The Deep," which also captured nods in six other categories. Seemingly a minor awards show, the Billboard Awards were nonetheless important in that they were chart position and data driven, which indicated that Adele had truly arrived as a viable commercial performer.

Adele's rise to the level of pop culture icon had long been assured. But it would seemingly take an established entity to make Adele's status. Fan magazines and Web sites were one thing, but when *TIME* magazine weighed in . . . that made the coronation complete.

In an announcement made in late April, the annual 100 Most Influential People in the World list had Adele on it. The honor was tinged in irony as pop star Pink, who had long ago influenced Adele in the direction of pop music stardom, tweeted congratulations to the singer on the *TIME* magazine Web site.

"Turn on any radio station in the world and you'll probably hear Adele," she said. "I'm always so happy when the world catches onto something great. Especially when it's authentic talent and great songwriting."

An amusing counter to Adele's *TIME* honors was quick in coming when Adele beat out Lady Gaga for the title of most popular Gay Icon in a very informal radio poll conducted by the organization Gaydar.

XL would benefit from Adele's success in the Music Life Awards held in late April. The label would collect awards for Best A&R, Best Artist Marketing Campaign for *21*, Best Record Company, and Outstanding Contribution to XL boss Richard Russell. Adele was on hand to present Jonathan Dickins with Manager of the Year honors.

"I made my mind up that I wanted him to manage me," she said as she presented the award to Dickins. "Thank God I did because he's gone on to smash it."

While only recently settled in her Brighton Beach home, Adele continued to explore other living opportunities. In late April it was reported that the singer was looking for a family home in the West Sussex section of London, reasoning that she would also need a base of operations in the city for her career. Reports were that she was ready to pay out 10 million pounds in cash for the right property and that she was looking for a property in the high rent district . . .

Miles away from Tottenham.

The suspense on where or when Adele would once again sing in public was broken when Mumford & Sons lead singer Marcus Mumford and his girlfriend, actress Carey Mulligan, could not hold back the news that Adele was going to sing at their wedding, which would take place the weekend of April 21. It was not known whether the singer would sing a selection of her own songs or classics from other people.

What made it worldwide news was that Adele was breaking her post-Grammy/BRIT silence and was going to sing again.

As expected, this sudden step back into the limelight, even on such a small scale, once again had the media on fire with the speculation that Adele, as only the singer could, was possibly making a first tentative step back into the limelight. Or, quite simply, this could merely be a one-off favor for a dear friend.

Within twenty-four hours of the announcement, reality set in and Adele did not sing at the wedding.

April turned to May. Adele would be celebrating her twenty-fourth birthday on May 5. The singer's birthday would also mark the culmination of nearly a quarter of a century that had seen Adele's life and career go from the very bottom to the heights of worldwide acclaim. The future would begin with that birthday. So what does one get the megastar who has everything?

Perhaps a marriage proposal.

20

THE END...FOR NOW

A dele's is a life in progress. Consequently, there may be a door or two closing on her past and present. But there is always the future to consider. And hope for.

We all wish her the best and, yes, it's selfish. If Adele is in the right frame of mind, her voice will soar, her music will sing, and we will all be happy in a world where Adele's music is the sound track. But this is reality and so, while we hope and pray for all good things, there are some serious questions that need to be entertained.

Unless her latest relationship unexpectedly fails (and all indications are that they are in it for the long haul), Adele's future musical life will be driven by happiness. Can Adele translate a happy ending into emotional music with the ease that she was able to with heartbreak? Will the legions of fans that have lived by her passion follow her into the land of sweetness and light? Or can Adele find new ways of expressing the quiet and solitude that have brought her to this point?

There is a lot to consider. Can Adele's voice truly survive the rigors of performing live, or was her Grammy performance literally a last hurrah? She wants a family and is planning on lots of children. How will that impact a career that is in its second stage and will need the kind of constant attention that Adele may not have it in her to give? Pop is a fickle mistress, one whose supporters have notoriously short attention spans and require constant attention to keep them interested. Will Adele be able to have a career and life on her terms? Or will she wake up someday to find the people who loved her have moved on to the next big thing?

Tough questions. But questions that need to be asked if you have, in a space of a few years, traveled the road from obscurity to the top of the mountain. Questions that need to be answered.

Quite simply, Adele is too much of a legitimate talent to supernova out in a few years. There should be so much more and there just might be . . . if Adele can continue to have it on her terms.

But one thing is certain. However the rest of Adele's life and career play out, it's been one hell of a ride. Thanks, Adele, for the good times.

DISCOGRAPHY

ALBUMS

19

Release Date: January 28, 2008
Songs: "Daydreamer," "Best For Last," "Chasing Pavements," "Cold Shoulder," "Crazy For You," "Melt My Heart To Stone," "First Love," "Right As Rain," "Make You Feel My Love," "My Same," "Tired," "Hometown Glory."

21

Release Date: January 22, 2011 (UK), February 22, 2011 (US)
Songs: "Rolling In The Deep," "Rumor Has It," "Turning Tables," "Don't You Remember," "Set Fire To The Rain," "He Won't Go," "Take It All," "I'll Be Waiting," "One And Only," "Lovesong," "Someone Like You."

Live At the Royal Albert Hall

Release Date: November 28, 2011 (UK), November 29, 2011 (US)

Songs: "Hometown Glory," "I'll Be Waiting," "Don't You Remember," "Turning Tables," "Set Fire To The Rain," "If It Hadn't Been For Love," "My Same," "Take It All," "Rumor Has It," "Right As Rain," "One And Only," "Lovesong," "Chasing Pavements," "I Can't Make You Love Me," "Make You Feel My Love," "Someone Like You," "Rolling In The Deep."

EXTENDED PLAY ALBUMS

Live from Soho

Release Date: February 3, 2009

Songs: "Crazy For You," "Right As Rain," "Make You Feel My Love," "Melt My Heart To Stone," "Hometown Glory," "Chasing Pavements," "Fool That I Am," "That's It, I Quit, I'm Moving On."

iTunes Festival London

Release Date: July 14, 2011

Songs: "One And Only," "Don't You Remember," "Rumor Has It," "Take It All," "I Can't Make You Love Me," "Rolling In The Deep."

SINGLES

"Hometown Glory"

Release Date: October 22, 2007

"Chasing Pavements"
Release Date: December 7, 2007
"Cold Shoulder"
Release Date: March 30, 2008
"Make You Feel My Love"
Release Date: November 3, 2008
"Rolling In The Deep"
Release Date: November 29, 2010
"Someone Like You"
Release Date: January 23, 2011
"Set Fire To The Rain"
Release Date: July 4, 2011
"Rumor Has It"
Release Date: March 15, 2012

FEATURED ARTIST

"My Yvonne"
Recorded with Jack Peñate in 2007. Appears on the album
Matinee.

"Many Shades Of Black"
Recorded with The Raconteurs in 2008. Appears on the album *Consolers Of The Lonely*.

"Water And A Flame"
Recorded with Daniel Merriweather in 2009. Appears on
the album *Love & War*.

"Every Glance"
Recorded with Jack Peñate in 2009. Appears on the album
Everything Is New.

"Make You Feel My Love"
A live recording from radio station WXPN. Appears on the charity album *Chimes Of Freedom: Bob Dylan, Honouring 50 Years Of Amnesty International.*

SONGS IN MOVIES

"Chasing Pavements"
In the movie *Wild Child* (2008).
"Right As Rain"
In the movie *I Love You, Man* (2009).
"Make You Feel My Love"
In the movie *When in Rome* (2010).
"Hometown Glory"
In the made-for-television movie *Der Mann auf der Brücke* (2009).

SONGS IN TELEVISION

"Chasing Pavements"
In the Season 1 episode of *90210* entitled "We're Not In Kansas Anymore."
"Daydreamer"
In the Season 1 episode of *90210* entitled "The Jet Set."
"Don't You Remember"
In the Season 2 episode of *The Vampire Diaries* entitled "Daddy Issues."
"Hometown Glory"
In the Season 1 episode of *Secret Diary of a Call Girl*.

In the Season 5 episode of *One Tree Hill* entitled "Life Is Short."

In the Season 4 episode of *Grey's Anatomy* entitled "Freedom."

In the Season 1 episode of *90210* entitled "Love Me or Leave Me."

In the Season 5 episode of *The Hills* entitled "It's On, Bitch."

"Make You Feel My Love"

In the Season 2 episode of *Lipstick Jungle* entitled "Lover's Leaps."

In the Season 3 episode of *Brothers & Sisters* entitled "Missing."

In the Season 4 episode of *Ghost Whisperer* entitled "Thrilled to Death."

In the Season 7 episode of *One Tree Hill* entitled "Every Picture Tells a Story."

In the Season 2 episode of *Parenthood* entitled "Qualities and Difficulties."

In the Season 1 episode of *Hellcats* entitled "Before I Was Caught."

In the Season 6 episode of *Bones* entitled "The Change In the Game."

In the Season 3 episode of *Parenthood* entitled "My Brother's Wedding."

"One And Only"

In the Season 1 episode of *Unforgettable* entitled "Up In Flames."

"Right As Rain"

In the Season 2 episode of *Lipstick Jungle* entitled "Pandora's Box."

In the Season 3 episode of *Ugly Betty* entitled "In the Stars."

"Rumor Has It"

In Season 7 of *Grey's Anatomy* in the episode entitled "This Is How We Do It."

In Season 1 of *The Lying Game* in the pilot episode.

In Season 1 of *Ringer* in the episode entitled "That's What You Get for Trying to Kill Me."

In Season 1 of *Pan Am* in the episode entitled "Secrets and Lies."

In Season 1 of *Smash* in the episode entitled "The Cost of Art."

"Someone Like You"

In Season 4 of *The Secret Diary of a Call Girl*, episode 8.

In Season 7 of *Grey's Anatomy* in the episode entitled "This Is How We Do It."

"Turning Tables"

In Season 6 of *Criminal Minds* in the episode entitled "Coda."

SOURCES

It goes without saying that Adele's life and times have been the subject of in-depth scrutiny by the most diligent entertainment and celebrity journalists on the planet. Their professionalism in discovering everything there is to know about Adele is applauded. Many thanks.

The following newspapers helped make it all possible: *The Daily Mail, The Sun, New York Post, The New York Times, The Guardian, Star, USA Today, New Zealand Herald, The Scotsman, The Observer, The Independent, The Telegraph, Minneapolis StarTribune, New Musical Express, Scottish Daily Record, Calgary Sun, The Mirror, The West Australian, Interview, The Juice, Los Angeles Times, LA Weekly, Vancouver Sun, The Sunday Times, The Washington Post, South Wales Evening Post, Illinois Entertainer, News Of The World, Variety, Manchester Evening News, The Advertiser, The Lancashire Telegraph.*

These magazines made all the difference: *US Weekly, Vogue, BlackBook, Cosmopolitan, Out, Platforms, Blues & Soul,*

Billboard, Heat, We Out Here, People, Rolling Stone, American Songwriter, G Magazine, Elle, Time, Time Out London, Entertainment Weekly, M Magazine, New York Fashion, OK Magazine.

The following Web sites came through with flying colors: Spyder's Random Things, Gather, Adele's Official Website, Adele Wiki, Reuters, MSN Music, Clash Music, TwitLonger, Stuff, IDI Newsletter, Hollywire, Pollstar, Hitquarters, Interviews And Gig Reviews, Adele TV, Hits 102.7, Song On Lyrics, CoolFM, National Public Radio, Spinner, The Huffington Post, Adele Quotes, Aceshowbiz, Capitol FM, The Free Library, ABC News, News Now, Postnoon, RTE Ten, Contact Music, Anatomy Of A Music Video, Music Week, Tune Find, BBC Newsbeat, NRJ Radio, Blogcritics, CBS Sunday Morning, Entertainmentwise, E Music News And Features, Softpedia, Bluegrass Today, Associated Press, Digital Spy, CMT, MTV, Pop Matters, The Story Behind The Song, Celebitchy, Express, Scenta, Great Personalities, 411 Mania, Black Entertainment, MOG, Artists Direct, Idolator, KSHP, CanCulture, Bright Young Things, Female First, Flickering Myth, Radar On Line, Tweet My Song, Weeping Elvis, The Rhapsody, Pop Idol, Daily Motion, Showbiz Spy, My Play, PopEater, E Online, Entertainment Oneindia, AOL Music Sessions, Mindfood, PressParty, Diva Report, Sound On Sound, Sky Living, Behyped.